I Was Evicted From Earth!

...And So Were You.

To the planet Earth;
Thanks for putting up with us.

Prologue

In the beginning, there was nothing, and it was good. Or at the very least, it wasn't bad.

But then someone or something (depending on your philosophical beliefs) had to go and set off a big bang in the middle of all that peaceful nothingness, and the universe began to spread out across the floor like an overflowing bathtub.

Giant balls of burning gas called stars formed and began to gather into galaxies, and these galaxies spun and rotated around the center of the universe. Planets molded themselves from all the dust, debris, and gases that were still floating about, and they too began to spin and rotate around the already spinning and rotating suns. All in all, there was an awful lot of spinning and rotating going on, which might explain why the universe was such a dizzy place full of very dizzy creatures.

One typically dizzy such place, the planet Earth, rotated and spun in its own little corner, a lonely blue and green oasis in a vast, endless desert of more of the nothingness that there still seemed to be a helluva lot of. Its orbit was just near enough to the Sun to provide a temperate climate, (except for the areas that would someday be known as Las Vegas and Minnesota), and a rich, nurturing atmosphere covered the globe. And to make matters even worse for the poor Earth, there was plenty of thirst quenching water to be found on its surface, thanks to a plethora of icy comets that had clumsily crashed into it over the years.

In other words, whether it liked it or not, Earth was unlucky enough to be among the small minority of worlds that was perfectly suited to sustain life.

Soon lush, green plants sprung up and began to grow in abundance, helping to keep the atmosphere's delicate balance in check. Billions of furry, feathered, scaly, and skinned animals scurried and swam about and ate the plants, as well as each other, once they got bored with a strictly vegetarian diet.

A food chain formed, and eventually the dinosaurs found themselves on top of it. It looked for a while as if they were the ones who were destined to build all the Starbucks, but a big rock intervened and hit the planet before any of the T-Rex got around to figuring out the wheel, or more importantly, outerwear. And since the bulk of the thunder lizards were too lazy to quickly evolve into something with feathers or fur, their most advanced creation before they all froze to death turned out to be a giant pile of dino dung. Everything fell back into a state of animal chaos, and for a while, all plans for overpriced coffee shops were put on hold.

But civilization was determined to exist, and scrawny, two legged creatures called humans were the next and best idea evolution could come up with. And while they weren't nearly as cool as the dinosaurs, they were at least every bit as hell bent on killing one another and any other creature that got in their way, so they did have their upside.

These humans quickly set out to improve things, excavating stone and metal to build giant cities in order to get on their neighbor's nerves more efficiently. They found coal under their feet and dug it up and burned it to generate electricity, so they could condition the air and watch reality TV shows about one another. Walking began to seem awfully primitive, and they manufactured millions upon millions of automobiles to avoid this unnecessary exercise. And of course, all those cars had to run on something, so they sucked oil out of the ground. Which was great, because it gave them something new to fight over and spill into the oceans.

The Earth didn't mind all of man's improvements at first. It didn't have much to say in the matter anyway, being just a planet and all that. But it did have things set up a certain way, and when the humans kept adding chemicals to the air, soil, and water that had no business being there, while chopping down huge chunks of the oxygen providing forests, it began to toss out more and more hurricanes and blizzards like a cow swishing its tail to remove a biting insect. The Earth wasn't being mean; again, it was just a planet. But this was the only way it

7

knew to try and get things back into balance, and maybe, just maybe, let the humans know they were getting a little too rowdy up on the surface.

But humans being human, they ignored Earth's warning signs and continued bettering life. And while there was a fair amount of debate about actually doing something to save the environment, no one could find any rock solid proof it *needed* saving, other than vast stretches of polar ice caps melting and holes in ozone layers. The humans didn't see any good reason to get on the bus with a bunch of other annoying humans without said proof, especially when they all had such nice Humvees and Ram trucks with hemis sitting waiting for them in their driveways. So in spite of the efforts of a few pesky Al Gorean types, the planet had to limp along and provide the finest in human and animal care it could manage, while having a few hundred billion tons of pollutants pumped into its environment.

Then one day, not so long ago or in the future, depending on when you are, the Earth finally got a little outside help that would change things forever. And one human who was not really any differently different from the rest of the humans found himself unexpectedly and reluctantly smack dab in the middle of it all.

His name was Jake Williams, and the most important thing to know about him, at least as far as I'm concerned, is that he happened to be me.

Chapter 1

Let me just say upfront and for the record that I'm a city boy. I was born on concrete, grew up on concrete, and planned to die on concrete. I came into being in the heart of Chicago, and the few times I'd left her I'd stayed on concrete roads until I'd reached another concrete city, or had flown far over the top of any large patches of green in a fast moving metal jet.

I felt comfortable living in my dirty little satellite. A city is like a man made moon that's stuck to the planet's surface; it's a world unto its own, built to keep the planet beneath it out. Oh, it sticks through in places; a few trees along the street, or maybe a small yard or park here and there. But until you get farther out into the suburbs, it's more man than nature, and I liked it that way.

So I wasn't exactly the ideal candidate for the position that was thrust upon me. I didn't have anything against the birds and the bees and the flowers and the trees, but I wasn't in the habit of dancing naked with a goat in the middle of a field of clover under a full moon, either. So if I seemed more irritated than anything by the whole affair, you should now know why.

I suppose it was a Thursday morning that was was more or less the starting point of the whole thing. I was lying in my bed, and if I would have just stayed there all day like I should have, none of it ever would have happened, or at least it wouldn't have happened to me. But I didn't; instead an odd sensation came over me, almost like a primal fear, and I awoke with a start. I opened my eyes, and found a pair of green feline ones looking down at me.

"Damn it, Arthur!" I said. "I thought we talked about this. I promised not to get you fixed and you promised to stop scaring the hell out of me every morning."

My cat licked his lips and continued to stare at me from his position on my chest.

"Not to mention it makes me wonder how long you've been there and what you've been doing all this time," I said. "Probably performing some crazy cat ritual or something. Now scram and go do something useful, like finding that family of mice that keeps getting into my frosted flakes."

Arthur jumped off the bed and padded out of the room, his mission accomplished.

I rolled over and checked out my alarm clock, which read just past eleven. I smiled and stretched, feeling good about being able to sleep in on a Thursday, even if it meant I had a three hour drive ahead of me. I got up and went into the bathroom and did all the things necessary to interact with other humans without having them recoil in disgust, then packed a few toiletries, which

I carried along with the rest of my previously suit-cased belongings into the living room.

I went into the kitchen and whipped up a quick breakfast of fruit, oatmeal, and toast, then sat down and ate, while reading the paper and discussing the news with Arthur.

"It says here we're in for some warm weather again this weekend; good time for me to be getting out of Chicago," I said. "Of course, you'll be staying here and chilling in the central air. You wouldn't like it where I'm going anyway; I don't know if they have fluoridation, so the toilet water would probably taste funny to you. Besides, I don't want you running around with all those country cats, then coming back here and line dancing or something."

My fat orange tabby meowed a complaint.

"It's not like I'm leaving you here all on your own, you know," I said. "Ms. Angela from across the hall is going to come over and take care of you. If you play your cards right and look a little lonely, she might take you over to her place and you can spend some quality time with her Siamese that I know you've had your eye on. Just be safe. You don't want to get tied down with a wife and kittens. Trust me, it always ends the same; she'll get the litter box and all your cat toys in the settlement, and you'll be left sitting here all alone, getting looped on catnip to ease the pain."

Believe me, I knew a little about such things, being one of Chicago's most up and coming divorce lawyers. At twenty-nine I already had a thriving practice which had netted me a nice, plush apartment, a custom Humvee, and more than a few dates with lawyer wife wannabees. My biggest worry was usually where to have dinner and drinks, although I had to admit that enduring some of the more brutal marital breakups I refereed often made me look forward to the drinking part of the evening more than the dining. But overall, I still considered myself a pretty successful and happy single guy without much of a care in the world.

I got up and put my dishes in the dishwasher, then pulled a gray sports jacket over the black tee and tan slacks I was wearing. I picked up my bags and went over to the door, opened it, and stopped to say goodbye to Arthur.

"So look, I'll be back in a few days unless something goes wrong and they need me for a quick divorce right after the wedding," I said. "And you better still be single when I get back." Arthur gave me a *"go already so I can start getting into things"* look, and I exited the apartment, closed and locked the door, and took the elevator down to the parking garage.

I walked across the pavement towards my beloved black Humvee, and pushed the button on my car remote. The alarm chirped back at me and unlocked the doors, and moments later I turned the key and the engine roared to life, and we exited the garage into heavy traffic on Twenty-Third Avenue.

My trusty mount and I battled our way from the heart of downtown, past the Picasso and Wrigley Field, then inched our way out of the Chicago metropolitan area and into the Milwaukee metropolitan area. We turned west and eventually found the open highway and began to make some time, while I conducted business on my iPhone. Time ticked slowly away, farm after farm whizzing by, as we exited onto smaller and smaller roads, until at last a friendly sign appeared that read, "*Welcome to Annandale.*"

I rumbled down the tiny main street in my urban-turned-rural assault vehicle, spotted what I was looking for, and pulled into an open parking spot. I got out of the car, took off my sunglasses, and looked around and smiled, a little amused at the quaint scene before me. "Welcome to Mayberry; this is usually all in black and white," I thought. "I wonder what Deputy Fife is up to."

It was a beautiful, warm summer's day in the little farm town of Annandale, Wisconsin. People went about their daily business, making their way in and out of the small stores along the tree lined street. Most gave me a friendly smile or hello as they passed me by, but there were a few that stared at me like I was from another planet. Which I suppose I was, if you compared Chicago to Annandale.

The door to *Anderson Family Law* opened, and my friend Steve Anderson emerged wearing a maroon polo shirt and a pair of jeans. He waved and came towards me, and I smiled and waved in reply.

"Jake! You made it. Guess my directions got you here," said Steve.

"Yeah, they were a big help," I said. "Drive to Annandale, then stop the car."

"Hey it worked, didn't it? Great to see you, buddy," said Steve. We shook hands and gave each other a manly hug.

"So this is your new office, huh?" I said, motioning towards the little nearby brick building next to where I'd parked. "Any big cases yet? Gonna help Oly get custody of his blue ribbon hog from Lena?"

"Ha ha," said Steve. "I suppose you're going to start in with the small town jokes right away?"

"Yeah, I can't think of any reason to wait," I said.

"Great; looking forward to it," said Steve. "So how was the drive?"

"Long, and full of cows," I said.

"That's Wisconsin for you," said Steve.

"Made me hungry," I said.

"You wanna go grab a bite to eat?" asked Steve.

"Yeah, man. They got a McDonald's here?" I said.

14

"Nope," said Steve.

"Burger King?" I asked.

"Nada," said Steve.

I put my sunglasses back on and looked down over them at Steve. "All that beef roaming around the countryside and I can't get a burger?" I said. "I mean you do eat here, don't you? Aside from all the barbecuing."

"Usually we eat over at the diner," said Steve. He started to walk down the sidewalk. "This way; it's just down the street."

I looked around me, then followed. "Of course it's just down the street," I said. "If it wasn't just down the street, it'd be out of town, wouldn't it? Steve?"

We sat in a booth by the window in the small, old fashioned diner. A hand-made sign advertised the Wednesday night spaghetti feed. A few customers ate at tables around the room and on bar stools at the counter. Steve read a copy of the local newspaper while I finished off my cheeseburger.

Steve was an average looking, likeable guy in his late twenties, about five foot ten with brown hair. There was nothing that stood out about him and he tended to blend into any crowd, but he made everyone around him feel at ease, and people always remembered the nice guy they'd met at the party. He and I had been best friends ever since we'd attended law school together in Chicago some years ago. I liked him a lot, but he did have one annoying trait.

"Man, we are so doomed," said Steve, while looking at the paper.

"Not the doomed thing again," I groaned.

"Well, we are," said Steve.

"So you keep saying. What now?" I said.

"Take a look at this," said Steve, handing me the newspaper.

I took it and read out loud. "*One day only; all sofas and recliners thirty percent off,*" I said, then looked out the window. "You're right, Stevie; I think I see the Four Horsemen coming down Main Street."

"Not that, you idiot," said Steve. "Further down."

I read from the newspaper again.

"*Corn prices in May down three percent from April,*" I said. "Good thing I had my money in pork bellies."

"Give me that," said Steve, exasperated. He reached over and snatched the paper out of my hands, and swatted me on the head with it.

"This," he said. "*Scientists report that last week a twenty-three mile long strip of the arctic shelf broke off near Greenland.*"

"So?" I said.

"So? That's huge! That's almost from here to Appleton. Imagine if *that* fell into the ocean," said Steve.

"Man, that'd be a whole lot of cows," I said. "Hey, can cows swim?"

"They can but-" began Steve.

"Phew. That's a load off my mind," I said.

"Look, forget about the cows," said Steve. He shook the newspaper at me. "Doesn't this worry you? I mean, this is going on all the time; the temperature just keeps on rising."

"Good," I said. "Maybe someday we won't have to freeze our asses off when we make it to a Bears game."

"Packers game," said Steve.

"Whatever," I said. "Look, the point is, all this global warming stuff is probably just Mother Nature going through one of her cycle things."

"And if it isn't?" said Steve.

"Then there's gonna be a whole lot of bronze women with uber tans running around the Midwest," I said.

"Man, you're hopeless," said Steve.

"You keep saying that too," I said.

Steve had always been a worry wart. Me, I never saw the point. I figured if something bad was going to happen, I didn't need to make it worse by ruining the moments leading up to it, too. Ignore it 'til it happens then forget it right after it does, that's my motto. I'm not saying I don't care about anything, just that I don't usually stop and think about it long enough to find out.

Steve put the newspaper down. "So how have you been, Jake? Still bleeding the soon to be divorced dry?"

"That's what us divorce lawyer vampire types do," I said. "You still getting married?"

"This Saturday. Nice of you to show up, by the way," said Steve.

I reached into my jacket pocket and took out a business card holder, then opened it and took out one of my cards and slid it across the table towards Steve. "Here's my card. I'll give you my friends discount."

Steve gave the card and I a dirty look, and I laughed.

"No, seriously; I'm sure you two will do fine," I said. "Besides, you have my number already if you need it."

"Unless Cynthia erases it; she thinks you're a bad influence," said Steve.

"And I didn't think she liked me," I said. I stood and picked the check up off the table, got out my wallet, and put the bill and some greenbacks on the table. "I got this."

Steve got out of the booth and stood up. "Thanks, Jake," he said.

"No problem. You're getting married; you're gonna need all the money you can get," I said. I went out the door to the street and Steve followed.

"So this is really it, huh?" I said, stopping out on the sidewalk. "You're actually going to get married and practice law here in Smallville, and chase tractors instead of ambulances?"

"Something like that," said Steve.

"I guess I just don't get it. One minute you're living in Chicago working for a small and almost prestigious law firm, well on your way to a trophy wife, and suddenly you meet a horticulture student and you're head over heels in love with a 4H Club member," I said.

"That's how it happens sometimes; Cynthia's a great gal," said Steve.

"I'm not saying she isn't. But couldn't she be an even greater gal and move to Chicago where all the action is?" I said.

"The family farm is here," said Steve. "Since Cynthia's parents passed away last year, well; there was just no way she was moving to Chicago. Besides, I like it here too, Jake. It's peaceful. You should try it for a while."

"Sorry, I don't look good in overalls or hunter's orange," I said. "As soon as I get you all shackled up I'm going to see how fast I can get back to Chicago, where the cars are honking, the money's flowing, and the women all have long legs."

"Hey, Steve," said a rather attractive female voice that made my libido want to know who it belonged to. I turned and found its owner was a tall, overly attractive red-head wearing a blue halter top and cut-off jeans, the latter of which were pasted over the top of a pair of lengthy tanned legs.

"Hey, Paula," said Steve, as the woman walked past.

Paula gave Steve a little wave and looked me up and down, then turned and sashayed up the street.

I watched her stroll away with interest, marveling again at the simple wonders of denim.

"You were saying something about women having long legs in the big city?" said Steve.

"Yes I was, and yes, she did have some, two of them in fact. But if she and I lived together in a town this small, you *know* she'd just turn out to be my cousin," I said.

"Like that would stop you," said Steve.

"Good point," I said. "So what are we doing again tonight?"

"You're the one that's supposed to know. You are the best man," said Steve.

"My plan got nixed," I said.

"Cynthia didn't think it was a good idea," said Steve.

"Uh-huh. And what are we doing instead of my proposal?" I said.

"We're going bowling for starters," said Steve.

"Yeah, that beats the hell out of being carted around Chicago in a limo to watch gorgeous women toss their clothes around the room," I said. "And I could have sworn I'd made my feelings about bowling abundantly clear to you."

"You have, but it's time for you to face your fears," said Steve. He slapped me on the shoulder. "Come on; let's go get you settled in at the ranch. Then it's party time."

"Let's just hope things don't get too wild," I said. "I've heard Sheriff Taylor can be a real hard ass when he gits his dander up."

Chapter Two

It was a busy night at Bill's Bar, Bowling and Karaoke. Bill stood behind the bar making drinks, and a cute blonde waitress named Shelly moved through the room delivering them. Steve was up at the bar getting a round of beers for us while talking to Paula, the woman we'd seen earlier on Main Street.

I stood in lane three, bowling ball in hand, deep in concentration. I took aim, stepped forward, and gracefully rolled the ball towards the pins. And as usual, it curved off immediately to the left like it had a mind of its own, bouncing straight into the gutter. I gave the alley a dirty look, then turned and walked back towards Tommy and Craig.

"A little more to the right, Jake," said Tommy, a red-haired, freckled faced young man who Steve had stuck with the thankless task of being his usher.

"Hey, how am I supposed to bowl with him singing?" I said, while gesturing towards Mark, a slightly chunky man in a cowboy hat who was another member of the wedding party. Mark was up at the karaoke machine, microphone in hand, belting out a drunken, off-key version of *"I've Got Friends In Low Places."*

"Concentrate," said Craig, another of Steve's local friends, who was blonde and fit the mold of the average mid-western Norwegian.

"I am concentrating; at least as much as I can while wearing someone else's shoes," I said.

I waited for my ball to pop out of the ball return from wherever it disappeared to, and started towards my lane, but saw a small boy was ready in four and motioned for him to go first. The kid rolled his ball slowly down the lane granny style and got a strike, and went into a lengthy celebration dance. I looked at him sideways and stepped up, determined not to be outdone by a six year old, then rolled and managed to knock down the ten pin. I went and sat down and gave my red and green shoes an accusatory look; "It's all your fault," I said to them.

Steve walked down from the bar with a handful of beers and handed one to me. "Game over?" he asked. "What did you end up getting?"

"You mean, besides athletes foot?" I said. I pointed up to where the scores were projected. "It's right up there on the screen where everyone in America can see it; no secrets in bowling."

Steve checked out my total. "You're getting better. At least you scored higher than your age that time," he said.

"I see you ran into that redhead again," I said, changing the subject to one I could care more about.

"Who, Paula?" said Steve. "She asked about you, ya know. She said you were hot."

I scanned the bar and found Paula was still there, looking our way. "She probably hasn't seen anything this refined her whole life, the poor thing."

Paula waved, and I flashed my best smile and gave her a cute little wave back. Then she picked up a brown paper bag and headed towards the exit.

"Damn, she's getting away!" I said.

"Don't worry, you'll see her again. She's in the wedding," said Steve. "She just stopped by to pick up some wine coolers for Cynthia's bachelorette party."

"She's in the wedding?" I asked. "You really should tell me these things sooner. It should be like, *"Hey, Jake, we're going bowling, but there's going to be this hot, sexy woman in the wedding party."* You know, to keep my happy scales balanced."

"I'll see what I can do in the future," said Steve.

Mark finished singing and came down to join us. "What did you think of my song, Jake?" he asked.

"I think the Japanese sure got even with us for the atomic bomb with the whole karaoke thing," I said, taking a sip of my beer.

"That's what I like about you, Jake," said Mark. "You're a funny guy. Isn't he a funny guy, Tommy?"

"Very funny guy," agreed Tommy.

"Yeah; very funny guy," said Mark. "Shelly!" he shouted. "Another round of shots over here!"

Johnny, the local skateboarder, walked by at that moment, finished with the video game he'd been playing over in the corner. "Dude! Did I hear something about shots?" he said.

"And one for Johnny," yelled Mark.

"Thanks, dude!" said Johnny.

"How's it hanging, Johnny?" asked Steve.

"Couldn't be better, dude!" said Johnny. "Pulled a backside Nollie 360 on my board today; it was totally gnarly!"

"Sounds bitchin'," I said.

"Totally, dude," said Johnny.

"Johnny, this is Jake Williams; he's here from Chicago to be my best man," said Steve. "Jake, Johnny."

Johnny and I exchanged a complicated handshake. "Good to meet you, bro," said Johnny.

"Dude," I said.

Johnny was twenty-three years old and still lived with his mother. He had long, blondish hair that stuck out from under the red bandanna he always wore on his head. His Tony Hawke t-shirt was missing it's sleeves, and his ratty blue jeans were missing their knees. He was on the short side and stayed slender due to his busy schedule, despite a healthy diet of Snickers bars, nacho cheese Doritos, and Red Bull. He skateboarded in the afternoon, partied in the evening, played video games all night, then slept through the morning before starting the whole cycle over again. With so many full days it was no wonder he rarely found time for mundane tasks like work.

Shelly arrived with the shots and put them on the table. "You can bring the tab too, Shelly," said Steve.

"You guys leaving already?" said Shelly.

"Yeah, we leaving *already*?" I said..

"Sorry to break your heart," said Steve. He turned to Shelly. "Ignore Jake; he's fun impaired."

Shelly looked at me. "Too bad," she said, then left to get our bill.

The guys gathered around and picked up their shots, and Craig raised his to make a toast. "To Steve and Cynthia," he said. "May the road go uphill to meet you. No wait. May the wind behind you always...no, that's not it either. Okay; how about this; may you never find Cynthia in the back seat of a Chevy with-"

"Nip it!" I said, interrupting him. "We'll just nip that in the bud; sit down before you hurt someone. Got to do everything around here myself." I thought for a moment before speaking. "May your life together with Cynthia be filled with all the happiness, warmth, and love the world can give you."

I paused as if finished, and everyone started to drink, but stopped as I continued again.

"And when that runs out, be sure and give me a call before Cynthia does, or I'll make sure she gets your truck in the divorce," I said.

Everyone clinked their glasses together and cheered, then drank down their shots.

Steve came over to me, feigning teary eyed and sniffling. "That was beautiful, man. I love you," he said, then tried to give me a big hug.

I put up my hands to defend myself. "Hey, hey now! None of that," I said. "No manly hugs tonight, please. And you think you're crying now, just wait till you're married."

Shelly came over with the tab and I got out my wallet and paid her, while everyone grabbed their belongings and prepared to leave.

"You know, you don't have to pay for everything, Jake," said Steve.

I pointed at myself. "Divorce lawyer," I said, then pointed at Steve. "Pig lawyer."

"Can I come with you guys?" asked Johnny, hopefully.

"No!" said everyone in unison.

"Duuudes!" said Johnny, crestfallen.

"Sorry, man; I was pulling for you," I said.

Johnny wandered off to look for someone else to buy him a drink.

"Where are we going now?" I asked Steve.

"Bonfire time," said Steve.

"Out to the farm, huh?" I said. "Did you pick up marshmallows and graham crackers? And Hershey bars?"

"No, but we do have a keg," said Steve.

"Damn! Don't you know anything about bachelor parties? How are we supposed to make smores?" I asked.

"Come on, smart guy," said Steve as he went out the door.

"You can't have a wild and crazy bachelor party without smores!" I said.

Chapter Three

It was a gorgeous, clear, Wisconsin night, a darker version of the earlier day. A soft breeze blew through the trees as the crickets chirped happily away.

Cynthia's two story, Norman Rockwell country farm house sat near the road on the front edge of the property, a dirt driveway leading up to it. A porch wrapped around the house, complete with hanging swing. A white wooden fence ran along the edge of the big lawn, keeping the peacefully dozing black and white dairy cows out of the yard and in the pasture where they belonged.

A fire burned in a pit by the house, surrounded by lawn chairs. Steve and I sat next to one another, watching the fire and drinking Grain Belt Premiums.

I looked up at the sky, which looked vastly different here in the country. I could see the Milky Way, for instance, and if I wanted to gaze at that in Chicago I'd have to go into a Qwiki Mart and stare at the candy rack. "Nice night; that's one helluva lot of stars up there," I said.

Steve, who was moderately going on majorly intoxicated, tipped his chair back on two legs while rocking it. "Yeah, it sure is," he agreed.

"I gotta say this is nice; so quiet," I said.

"Glad you like it," said Steve.

"Speaking of quiet, where'd the rest of the boys go?" I asked.

"They went to say *"Hi"* to the cows," said Steve.

"You're kidding right? I bet if Cynthia finds out she's gonna be p.o.'d," I said.

"They're not messing with Cynthia's cows; they're way too afraid of her for that. They're over at Craig's place just down the road," explained Steve. "I doubt if we'll see them again tonight."

"I hope they all get sat on," I said. "I mean, I wonder how they'd like it? Poor cow is just standing there, snoozing away, dreaming about getting jiggy with some hot bull, and all of a sudden, *"Wham!"* she's lying on the ground wondering what the hell happened and how she's going to get back up again."

"I thought you didn't like cows," said Steve, yawning.

"I don't, but that doesn't mean I think someone should be knocking them over just because they're too stupid to lie down and sleep like everyone else," I said.

There was a quiet moment, and I stirred the fire with a stick while Steve leaned way back in his chair and looked up at the night sky.

"I think I see a UFO," said Steve.

I looked up. "Where?"

Steve tipped his chair too far back and fell with a clatter, legs flailing in the air, as I calmly watched.

"Never mind, it's just a satellite," said Steve, from his new position on the ground.

"You need some help?" I said.

"No, I think I'll just stay down here for a while," said Steve. "Kind of comfortable."

"Suit yourself," I said.

We sat quietly, Steve looking up at the stars through glazed eyes from his back, me contemplating whether or not it was a good time to be serious for a change, and deciding it was. "Hey, Steve," I said.

Steve yawned. "Hey, Jake," he said.

"I've got something I've been wanting to say to you," I said.

"Go for it," said Steve.

"You know how I always give you grief about getting hitched to Cynthia, and all that?" I said.

"You mean, like the time you tied me to a chair and threatened to shave off my mullet if I didn't come to my senses and break off the engagement?" asked Steve sleepily.

"No, that was actually pretty stupid," I said. "If you would have come to your senses I wouldn't have shaved off your mullet like I did. Then I would have had to turn around and tie you back to the chair again until you came to your senses and let me shave off your mullet."

"What are you talking about, then?" said Steve, barely audible.

"All those other times," I said. "Saying you were making a big mistake marrying Cynthia. Telling you you were out of your mind and should stay in Chicago; although I still think the two of you should do that part."

I paused to wait for Steve to say something, but he didn't.

"I just wanted to say I was wrong; about everything but Chicago, anyway. And to tell you I'm happy for you," I said. "You know, finding someone to spend your life with. Raising a family, all that jazz. You're my best friend and I want the best for you. I love you man."

There was still no answer from Steve.

"You've got the right idea. I mean, all I have is an endless stream of gorgeous women going in and out of my apartment. What kind of life is that for a guy?" I said. "And it's been making me wonder lately, at least a tiny little bit; maybe I should settle down too. Find the right girl like you did. Do you think I'm ready?"

Steve remained silent, and I looked down at him to see what was going on. "Yo, Steve?" I said.

Steve began to snore from where he lay on the ground.

"I'll take that as a no; thanks for the support," I said, and stood up. "Gonna go use the facilities; let me know if you need anything."

I walked away from the bonfire towards a small group of bushes next to the white pasture fence and stopped, then unzipped my fly and prepared to do my business. I was looking down, minding that business, when I heard an odd humming sound, quiet at first but gradually growing louder. It seemed to be coming from above me, so I looked up to see what it was. I squinted, not sure what I was seeing, then my eyes grew wide as I stared at the glowing light coming down from the sky.

I knew what it was right away, of course. I'd seen plenty of movies and knew if you were standing in the middle of nowhere, or at least close to it, and a light began to come down from the sky as this one was now, you pretty much had to figure it was a spaceship. That didn't mean I really believed what I was seeing, either, but there it was; a shiny, silver, perfectly round orb about fifty feet in diameter, lit with pulsating blue lights going on and off in sequence around the center of the ship.

I stared upwards at it in amazement, my face lit with a pale blue glow as the ship passed overhead. It floated quietly towards the pasture and descended closer and closer to the surface of the planet, then began to slow down, and as it did so, three beams of blue light emanated from its underside, forming a tripod of sorts.

The craft finally came to a gentle landing thirty or so yards away from me, floating about five feet off the ground, apparently held there by the beams of light.

Mesmerized, I walked over to the gate in the fence, opened it, and walked towards the ship, my mouth hanging open in awe. I stopped a short distance away and cocked my head to one side and stared, puzzled and unsure of what to do next.

I didn't have a lot of life wisdom in the area of UFOs. Show me a hot looking woman across the room and I could tell you how to approach her, but spaceships coming down from the sky, that was another matter. For what I paid for my degree you'd think they would have covered the subject more thoroughly in college, but I guess with all the cuts in education, first contact procedures and ethics was one of the first classes to go.

As I looked on and tried to decide what to do without the benefit of any outdated scholastic dogma, a silver metallic ramp about six feet wide elegantly slid outwards from the craft. It had curved sides like a water slide, and slowly extended itself all the way to the ground. An arched door materialized above the ramp, which slid open from bottom to top, and I shaded my eyes as bright light spilled from the interior. The outline of a small humanoid about five feet tall appeared in the doorway, and it moved down the ramp, carrying a small cylinder of some kind in its left hand.

The being wore no clothing, but since it was built like a doll it really had no need for it either, despite what clothes horses Ken and Barbie might think. It had bright yellow skin topped with no hair of any kind, mop top or eyebrow. Two cylindrically shaped solid black eyes bracketed a small nose above a small mouth, and tiny ears stuck out from its head.

The creature reached the bottom of the ramp and stopped to look around. It didn't seem to notice me, and instead walked towards a nearby cow and examined it, seemingly puzzled. "Are you sentient?" it asked.

The cow looked blankly back at him and chose not to answer, probably annoyed at having been awakened by the ship's lights.

"I said, are you sentient?" repeated the being, determined to illicit a response. It got none and appeared to become irritated, then looked around, its eyes coming to rest on me before moving towards me.

As the creature drew closer I suddenly began to wonder if remaining in the area had been that bright an idea. The little guy (or whatever he or she was) looked harmless enough, but then so did all the aliens in movies, right up to the point where they drew a laser pistol and melted your face to begin their campaign to wipe out your species and plunder your planet's resources. I thought about turning and running off to the farmhouse, or at least trying to rouse Steve for whatever help he might be, but found myself firmly riveted to the spot. The being came to within a few feet of me and stopped, looking me up and down while I did the same thing back.

"Are you sentient?" the alien asked.

For some reason it didn't occur to me to be offended by being quizzed in the same manner as a cow, and I simply said "What?" a bit dazed and confused by the whole thing, not to mention a little buzzed from all the celebratory shots and beers.

"Are you sentient?" asked the creature, annoyed at having to ask the same question for the fourth time in a row. "Do you know you exist and wonder why?"

"Yeah, I guess so," I said, uncertain of pretty much everything at this point.

"I wish he'd prep me better for these things," said the alien irritably. "It would have helped to at least know what you humans look like." It took hold of a thin metal rod running down the side of the cylinder it was carrying and pulled it out and away, and a lit screen pulled out behind it like an electronic scroll.

"Name?" asked the being.

"My name?" I asked.

"No, my name; I came all the way to your planet so we could stand here and play guessing games all night," said the alien sarcastically. "Of course your name!"

"Okay, okay," I said, a bit chagrined. "Jake."

"Jake; is that your first, middle and last name? Is it Jake Jake Jake or just Jake?" said the being.

"No, it's Jake Williams," I said.

The creature spoke while typing on the electronic scroll. "Social security number?" it said.

"Social security number?" I asked.

"Is there an echo in here?" said the being.

"You mean out here," I said, determined to get some control over the conversation.

"No, I mean in this environment. Don't correct me; unlike you creatures I always say what I mean," said the being. "Now give me your social security number."

"Fine. Seven-four-five, nine-two, four-eight-six-three," I said.

The being entered the numbers onto the pad, then moved towards me and held the scroll out while pointing at it. "Now place your right thumb onto the oval," it said.

I paused, looking at the brightly colored screen, then did as I was told. Don't ask me why; you would have done the same thing, given the circumstances. It's one of those things; when aliens land and tell you to put your thumb in an oval, you just do it.

The creature tapped on the scroll twice and pulled on the electronic page, and it came away from the rest of the cylinder and rolled itself into a neat tube similar to the original. The being handed it to me, and I reluctantly accepted it.

"What's this?" I asked.

"Your copy; you have been served. Have a nice day," said the alien. It turned and started walking back towards the ship.

"What?" I asked sharply, and the being stopped and turned back to face me.

"Have a nice day. Or night. Or not. Whichever you prefer," said the alien. It turned again and continued towards the ramp.

I shook myself and came out of the fog my head had been mired in. "Wait a minute! Hold it right there," I demanded. "What do you mean, I've been served?"

The being ignored me and moved across the pasture.

"You! Alien dude. I'm talking to you!" I said, louder this time. "What do you mean I've been served? Is that some sort of threat? Are you going to eat me now? Dip me in some methane based hot sauce?"

The little alien kept his back turned and went up the ramp.

"Come back here!" I shouted after him.

As the being reached the doorway of the ship it stopped and turned to face me. "By the way, your fly is open," it said, matter-of-factly.

I stared blankly at the alien, then looked down. "Damn it," I said, then fixed the problem. My first encounter with a little green man, maybe the first by any human, and I'd left the barn door open; no wonder he'd seemed impressed.

The being walked into the ship and the door slid shut behind him.

I stood breathing heavily from excitement, and stared at the craft. "Yeah, you better hide," I said.

Steve walked up behind me, yawning. "What's all the shouting about?" he asked.

"Well, what would you be doing if an alien just served you?" I asked.

"Depends on what was on the menu," said Steve, calmly.

I pointed at the ship. "Are you blind?"

"Oh that," said Steve, calmly dismissing it. "That's just part of my dream; go away and let me look for Jessica Alba."

I reached out slapped Steve hard across the face.

"Ow," said Steve, not so calmly.

"Yeah, ow," I said.

"Hey, that shouldn't hurt," said Steve.

"No, it shouldn't," I said. "And you shouldn't be dreaming about Jessica Alba anymore, either."

"You mean, this isn't a dream?" said Steve.

"Not unless it's mine," I said.

"So Jessica isn't going to wander by for no apparently good reason?" said Steve.

"No she isn't," I said. "But Cynthia might."

"Well, shouldn't we tell somebody?" said Steve.

"Who we going to tell? Your marriage counselor?" I said.

"Not about my dream!" said Steve.

"Oh, you mean tell someone about that alien space craft sitting over there next to your cows," I said.

"Yeah, that," said Steve.

"You got anyone in mind?" I said.

Steve thought for a moment. "I know. I'll call the sheriff," said Steve, turning and heading quickly towards the house.

"Good," I said, following. "Just be sure and tell him to give SETI a call because they might want to point a telescope or two at Cynthia's pasture."

We sat at the big wooden table in the farm house dining room. Or more precisely, Steve sat at the table while I slumped over it, my head lying on my arms as I tried desperately to stay awake, having finally given up on staring blankly at the daisies in the milk can centerpiece.

"Yes, that's right; a spaceship," said Steve into the telephone. "First contact made."

I yawned a little yawn.

"Look, I'm telling you the truth," said Steve after a short pause.

I yawned a slightly bigger yawn, and wondered if my king size bed in Chicago was missing me as much as I was missing it.

"So you believe me; good," said Steve. "But you're not going to come and do anything about it, are you?"

I fell asleep and woke back up five time in five seconds, and didn't feel refreshed by it in the least.

"Yeah. Yeah, I understand. Yep. Yep. Thanks a lot. You too; good bye," said Steve, and he hung up the phone.

"So?" I said sleepily, as opposed to in my sleep, which I would have preferred.

"So they don't care either," said Steve. "I've called the sheriff, the FBI, the CIA, NASA, the National Guard, and the Enquirer. They're all interested and say they believe we have a spaceship outside, but not enough to come here and do anything about it. Can you think of anyone else we could try?"

"We could call the Coast Guard, but we might be a little bit out of their jurisdiction," I said.

"What do you think is going on?" said Steve. "Why won't anyone come here?"

I sat up and rubbed my eyes. "Well, it is Wisconsin," I said. "All I know is it's weird, it's late, I'm tired, and I'm hung-over. I'm going to bed and hope this was all some sort of psychotic episode brought on by bowling."

"How can you sleep at a time like this?" asked Steve.

"What else am I supposed to do at a time like this? Go milk the cows?" I said, standing up. "No thank you; I don't want to shatter my illusion that milk comes from plastic jugs. Instead I'm going to lie down, close my eyes, and snore. I'll see you in a few hours." I walked out of the room and headed towards the stairs.

"Ten bucks says you won't be able to sleep!" Steve said after me.

"I'm telling Cynthia you've got a gambling problem," I said from the other room. "And don't touch that scroll!"

In my mind I could just see Steve reaching out and touching the scroll several times, then picking the thing up and examining it. "He never could keep his hands off my stuff," I said to myself.

Chapter Four

I lay peacefully sleeping in the comfy guest room, a big homemade quilt pulled up to my chin, as I drooled all over my pillow. Sunlight shown through the sheer curtains hanging over the window, and inched its way slowly across the floor.

I felt an odd sensation, almost like someone was watching me, and opened my eyes. "Damn it, Arth-" I began.

There was indeed someone watching me, but it wasn't my cat, since he was back in civilization. And it wasn't all the paintings of ducks that stared down at me from the walls that I sensed, either; instead it was an attractive brunette who sat in the overstuffed chair next to my bed. She was tall, with long, dark, wavy hair, and wore a white button down shirt and a pair of faded blue jeans. She had a natural beauty to her, one of those women who didn't have to try to be pretty; it just happened.

"Hi," I said, which wasn't the best opening line of my career, but was all I could muster at the moment.

"Hello," said the woman. "How did you sleep?"

"I don't know," I said. "I was too busy sleeping to notice." I looked the woman over and while I certainly didn't mind doing so, I was still perplexed. "Look, I don't want you to get the idea I don't like waking up with beautiful women in my room or anything, but who are you again?" I asked.

"Nicole Parks; maid of honor," she said.

I took a moment to verify I was wearing my sweat pants under the covers, then got out of bed and stood up. "Jake Williams; best man," I said. "Now we know who we are; just have to figure out what you're doing in my room."

Nicole pulled a digital camera out of her front shirt pocket and held it up. "I wanted to talk to you about the alien," she said. "I'm a photo-journalist; at least I'd like to be. Right now I work for the Milwaukee Post in classifieds. But that space ship out in the field might be my chance for a big break."

"You mean it's still there?" I said. I went over to the window and pushed the curtains aside and looked out. The ship did indeed stubbornly remain, unchanged, except now it was gleaming in the sunlight instead of the moonlight. "Damn. Bad enough it wasn't a dream; the least it could have done was flown away by now."

"Well it didn't, and since you were the one who made first contact last night I was hoping you'd let me follow you around and take some pictures," said Nicole. "You know, document what happens next."

I thought about it for a moment. "Okay. I'm about to go jump in the shower right now so if you want to follow me down the hall to the bathroom..."

"Uh, maybe we should start after that," said Nicole.

"Suit yourself. Thought you might want to snap some candids and get a leg up on USA Today," I said.

Nicole stood and went over to the doorway to leave the room. "Thanks for the offer, but no; I'll be waiting downstairs. If you're hungry, Cynthia's making a late lunch," she said.

"*Late* lunch?" I said, looking for my watch. "What time is it, anyway?"

"About three," said Nicole.

"Wow. Guess I was tired," I said, picking my suitcase up off the floor and putting it on the bed. "First contact must take something out of you."

Nicole started to go out of the room, then stopped halfway and leaned attractively against the door frame. "Yeah, Steve's been going crazy waiting for you to wake up; he wants to talk to you about that scroll," she said, then went out into the hallway.

"I knew it," I said, unzipping my bag. "I told him not to touch that."

Nicole put her head back inside the door. "Well, he did," she said, then left again.

I shook my head as I dug for something to wear. "Dude never listens to me. Even when I told him she was a he did he listen? Noooo."

Nicole popped her head in the doorway again and looked at me quizzically.

"Key West; spring break. Believe me, you don't want to know," I said.

Nicole pulled her head back out of the door and went downstairs, even though she probably did.

Steve sat at the table in the dining room looking refreshed, having himself slept for a few hours. He had the scroll pulled open and was reading it, a finished plate of food sitting in front of him. Nicole sat across from him drinking a cup of coffee.

I walked into the room and into the kitchen where Cynthia was busy making sandwiches, and went over to her and threw my arms open wide. "Cynthia! I didn't get to see you yesterday; how about a hug, girl?"

"It's afternoon, and why is there a spaceship sitting outside my house the day before I'm supposed to get married?" said Cynthia curtly, ignoring my request for a squeeze.

"Hello to you, too," I said. I gave up on schmoozing Cynthia for the moment and looked into the dining room, and saw Steve puttering around with the scroll. "Thought I told you not to mess with that thing."

"You know, I've been reading through this," said Steve. "It's a lot of legal mumbo jumbo..."

"Then shouldn't I be the one reading it?" I asked. "Never mind, I haven't had my coffee yet. Speaking of which..." I said, then poured myself a cup. I walked into the dining room and sat down across from Steve, next to Nicole.

"You forget I'm the one who got you through law school and all that legal mumbo jumbo," said Steve.

"Oh yeah. I just taught you how to pick up girls," I said, as Cynthia walked up beside me holding a plate of food. She gave me a dirty look, then plopped it down in front of me and went back into the kitchen. "Hey, it worked on you, didn't it?" I said after her. I picked up my ham and Wisconsin Cheddar cheese sandwich and took a bite, enormously hungry now that I was up and moving around. "So what is that thing, anyway?"

Steve glanced into the kitchen to make sure Cynthia was out of earshot, then leaned across the table. "Well, it's a little confusing and I don't get everything it's talking about, but I'm pretty sure it's an eviction notice," he said quietly. "From Earth."

"An eviction notice?" I hissed. "What, I'm being kicked off the planet?"

"No, *we* are," said Steve.

"What do you mean?" said Nicole.

"I mean you, me, Jake, George Bush, Johnny Depp; everyone," said Steve.

"Well, Georgie might have it coming," I said, grabbing a potato chip off my plate. "But get real, Steve; you must have read it wrong."

"I'm telling you, that's what it says," said Steve, motioning at the scroll.

"Give me that and let me take a look," I said, putting out my hand, then quickly taking it back again. "Never mind, the coffee still hasn't kicked in."

Cynthia walked through the room, heading towards the front door. "I'm going outside to make sure they're not vaporizing my livestock," she said, and disappeared.

Nicole heard the front door open and close, then said, "Don't you think we should let Cynthia in on this, too?"

"Of course," said Steve. "Just not quite yet. She's a wee bit tense about the wedding, and telling her our honeymoon might be on Pluto isn't liable to help much."

"Did the scroll say anything about *why* we're being evicted?" I asked.

"It's kind of sketchy on that point; something about some environmental report," said Steve.

"What do you think we should do, anyway?" I asked. "Since last night's phone calls suggested we're not going to get much help from any shady governmental organizations."

"I think you should go out and try to talk to them," said Steve.

"Me? Why me? I should only be going if you want me to try to get custody of the kids from them," I protested.

"Because it also says that the person served with this notice becomes the Representative of the Earth," said Steve. "I think that means you, buddy."

I put my sandwich down, good and annoyed to start my day. "Man, that's just great; you're too much of a wuss to have a real bachelor party, so I have to go off and talk to some smart-mouthed alien about why he thinks he can kick us off our planet, instead of trying to get a gorgeous stripper out of my apartment."

"Stripper?" said Nicole.

"Sorry; exotic dancer," I said.

"And I'm not a wuss," said Steve.

"Yes you are," I said. I sat stewing for a moment, then said "Well, Cynthia's not going to be happy if your wedding gets messed up because of all this and she loses out on some nice bath towels; she's liable to open up a whole case of whup-ass on the aliens." I picked up the rest of my sandwich and stood up. "Guess I better go see what I can do before the war of the worlds breaks out. Anyone want to come with me?"

"No," said Steve.

"Yeah, I forgot; you're a wuss," I said. "Nicole? Want to come and try to take the first in focus pictures of an alien?"

"Are you kidding? That would be great! Thanks for asking me, Jake," said Nicole.

"Don't mention it," I said. "At least now I won't have to die alone if they go all Independence Day on me."

Chapter Five

The spaceship sat unchanged, glittering in the Midwest sun like a new pickup truck. Cynthia stood watching it on the closest corner of the front porch as we came out the front door.

"I'll be over by Cynthia giving moral support," Steve said, and he walked towards his fiance.

"To who; me, you, or her?" I said, and Nicole and I continued on towards the ship as I munched on my sandwich.

"Where are you two going?" asked Cynthia, as we walked past under the porch.

"Just gonna go to clear up some things with the aliens, that's all," I said.

"Then tell them if they ruin my wedding I'm personally going to kick their a-" began Cynthia, before Steve reached over and covered her mouth with his hand.

"Okay; wasn't listed on my *"duties of the best man"* card, but oh well," I said. Nicole and I made our way to the pasture fence and opened the gate, and I stopped and popped the last bit of sandwich into my mouth and looked at the ship. I moved my head around in a circle to try to loosen up the developing kink in my neck, and said, "No pressure, Jake; you've just got to try to save the human race, that's all."

Nicole brushed the crumbs off my polo shirt, then we walked over to and up to the top of the shiny silver ramp. I paused and looked at Nicole for advice as to what to do next, and she shrugged, so I simply knocked on the spaceship door.

After a short moment a voice came as if from out of nowhere; "*Who is it?*" it said irritably.

"It's me," I said.

"*Me? I don't know any me's; go away,*" said the voice.

"No; let me in," I said. "Now." I narrowed my eyes and tried to look intimidating, which didn't make any much sense considering the fact the door was still closed and no one inside could see me anyway.

"What are you doing?" hissed Nicole.

"Being assertive," I said under my breath. "That sounds like the same alien from last night; he's not going to get the best of me again."

"Are you sure that's a good idea?" asked Nicole.

"No clue," I said.

"*This is your last warning; go away. Or else,*" said the voice menacingly.

"Or else what?" I asked.

"*Or else this,*" said the voice.

I stood alertly waiting for something nasty to happen while Nicole looked on nervously, but nothing zapped or pounced onto either one of us. I finally relaxed and shrugged, and at that moment my feet suddenly lost all connection with the metal surface and flew out from under me and I landed hard on my rump, and Nicole and I slid ungracefully down the ramp, ending up at the bottom in a heap, Nicole on top of me.

"*And stay off!*" said the voice.

"I'm so glad he didn't get the best of you this time," said Nicole, while trying to get her bearings.

"Turned out pretty good from where I'm lying," I said, not altogether displeased with my and Nicole's relative positions.

"What the heck happened anyway?" asked Nicole, her hair dangling down and tickling my face.

"Don't know. All of a sudden the ramp felt like a Chicago sidewalk in winter and we both went skating," I said. I locked eyes with Nicole's and found they were a lovely shade of brown. "I think we should hold this position for a while and plan our next move."

Nicole gave me a sideways look, then pushed herself up hard off my chest as I gasped, then stood and adjusted herself.

"Or not," I said, trying to catch my breath. I laid in the grass for a moment, looking up at the clouds, then hopped to my feet. "Let's try this again," I said. I stepped gingerly onto the ramp and found it was back to normal, then stomped up it as Nicole reluctantly followed. When I got to the top I banged as loudly and hard as I could on the door with my fist.

"*Now you're making me angry,*" said the voice. "*I told you to go away or-*"

Nicole and I grabbed at the sides of the ramp, expecting it to become slippery again. "Wait! Don't get all Teflon with the ramp yet. It's Jake," I said.

"*Jake? Just any Jake, or one Jake in particular?*" asked the voice.

"Just one Jake; the Jake you talked to last night," I said.

"*Oh, you,*" said the voice, sounding somewhat disappointed. "*The one letting the cows out of the barn.*"

Nicole gave me a funny look.

"Don't ask," I said. "Yeah, that Jake," I said to the disembodied voice.

"*Just one moment,*" answered the voice. There was a short pause, then the door to the spaceship slid open. "*You may enter.*"

"Yeah, we guessed that," I said. I looked back at the porch and Steve gave me a thumbs up sign, then we walked through the arched doorway and into the ship.

Chapter Six

The interior of the room we entered was completely empty. There was a wall that cut the ship down the middle, giving the room a half moon shape, with another arched door near one end of it. Every surface was gleaming silver, and it looked like HAL would have felt right at home. Soft, blue light emanated from strips running along the curved ceiling where it met the wall.

The door to the outside closed behind us as we entered, the little yellow being from the night before standing just inside the room with a sour look on its face. "I see we've rectified our little problem," it said sarcastically. "Or was that just part of the standard Earth greeting?"

"You know, for a little guy you have a pretty big mouth on you," I said.

"No, it is well within the universally accepted norm in proportion to my body," said the creature. "Wait here, and don't touch anything," it added before walking across the room towards the door, which slid open, then closed behind him as he exited.

I looked around me. "There's nothing to touch!" I shouted after the creature. "What do you think?" I asked Nicole.

"This is one big empty silver room," she said, while taking a picture of it.

"Maybe they haven't unpacked yet," I said.

The door slid open again, and a very large something, or more precisely someone, strolled through it. The someone was tall, about seven feet or so, with a large build. His skin was a soft purple in color. He had black hair with a blue tinge to it that was slicked down on his head, with bushy eyebrows the same color above dark blue eyes. His nose was angular and his ears big and pointy. He wore what looked to be a kind of business suit cut in sharp angles, the jacket and pants a deep iridescent blue, and the vest a dark iridescent purple. Instead of a tie around his thick neck he wore a white ascot of sorts, while all of his fingers sported rings set with colored gem stones of some kind. He walked across the room in a proud, upright fashion, and would have blotted out a good portion of the sun if one would have been present. Even without the eclipse I was impressed, not to mention a little intimidated, and Nicole and I stared openly at him as he approached.

"Salutations!" he said, in a deep, dignified voice.

"Huh?" I said, wondering if this is what guards in the NBA felt like when Shaq bore down on them.

The big purple giant looked at me quizzically, and evidently decided to try a simpler greeting. "Hello?" he said.

"Oh, yeah," I said, remembering finally how to communicate. "Hello. So you are..."

"Varcus Gromell, at your service," said the alien, putting out a giant hand towards me. I looked at it for a long second, thinking he could probably easily crush mine if he wanted to, then slowly took it and shook hands with him, my hand engulfed by his enormous mitt.

"I'm Jake," I said.

"Of course you are," said Varcus, warmly. He looked at Nicole. "And she is?"

I looked at my assistant and found her still staring up at Varcus, and waved my hand across her eyes. "In shock I think. Her name is Nicole."

"I get that a lot, I'm afraid," said Varcus, almost apologetically. "Won't you both sit down?"

I looked around me at the empty room. "Um, you want us to just hunker down somewhere?"

Varcus glanced around, then looked irritated and took out a small electronic device that looked like a PED (personal electronic device) from his top jacket pocket. "My apologies; the robot should have taken care of this."

"That yellow guy's a robot?" I asked.

"Well, to be precise, a biological humanoid simulator, but that's a mouthful," said Varcus, tapping on the PED.

"You might want to do something about his attitude," I said.

"Believe me, I've tried; it seems to be hard wired in. There, that should do it," said Varcus, while pressing a few more buttons on his device. A round table surrounded by three chairs rose up from the floor in the center of the room, like solid turning into liquid and then back again. One of the chairs was Varcus sized, large and high backed. The other two were smaller and shaped like an upside down J, as if the being sitting in them would have to sit on the underside of the top.

I walked over and examined one of the crazy chairs, then looked over at Varcus. "You expect us to sit on these? Because I didn't wear my jeans with the Velcro buttocks today."

"Oops," said Varcus. "Wrong species."

"Wow. I don't even wanna know," I said.

"Must have hit the Hootoo button. Lovely people. Except for the constant oozing of course," explained Varcus.

"Yeah, you gotta hate that," I said.

Varcus tapped on his PED again and the two chairs flowed into something more fitting for humans and an episode of Mod Squad. "There; that's better. And let's let in a little light too, shall we?" said Varcus. He pressed a couple of buttons and the round dome over our heads dissolved away. Nicole and I looked up, the sun beating down on our faces.

"That was a neat trick," I said.

"Yes, no point in being indoors on a summer's day on Earth. Please, be seated," said Varcus.

"Thanks," I said, and Nicole and I sat down. Varcus politely waited until the two of us were seated then did so as well, putting his PED down on the table in front of him and leaning forward, elbows resting on the table, his fingers interlaced.

Nicole held up her camera. "Would it be alright if I took some pictures of you?"

"Certainly! Go right ahead," said Varcus. Nicole snapped a couple shots of Varcus as he sat smiling at the camera, then took a few more of the ship.

I noticed I could see Steve and Cynthia on the porch now that the walls were gone and waved, but they didn't seem to see me, and I wondered if perhaps the walls were still there but only transparent from our perspective. When the pleasant breeze blew through my hair I decided to give up trying to figure it out and just went with it instead.

"So; what can I do for you?" asked Varcus.

It occurred to me that I had no idea where to begin. "Think you can get me started here?" I asked Nicole, who leaned over and whispered a suggestion into my ear. "Oh yeah; now I remember. Just what the hell do you think you're doing?"

"I beg your pardon?" said Varcus.

"That's not what I said," said Nicole.

"I liked mine better," I said.

"Perhaps if you could be more specific," said Varcus.

"Why are you barging into our farms handing out eviction notices to people?" I demanded. "And why me?"

"Ah. That," said Varcus.

"Yeah. That," I said.

"I'll answer the second part first. You because you were there," said Varcus.

"Meaning what?" I said.

"Meaning the landing spot was picked at random by a computer out of all the viable landing spots on Earth," explained Varcus. "Then I sent the robot out to find the first being he came across that he could serve the notice to; it just happened to be you. So you see, you were actually quite lucky."

"Boy, and I'm feeling it," I said. "Back to the first part."

"Certainly," said Varcus. He picked up his PED, tapped a button, and spoke into it. "Robot, please bring me GREEN's report," he said. "It should just be one moment. Is there anything you'd like to ask while we wait?"

"Yeah, that biological human dude. What exactly is he?" I said.

"He's my assistant," said Varcus. "He's able to move, think, sense, and eat. And sometimes even feel I suspect, although it wasn't part of his original programming."

"Almost like Rush Limbaugh," I said. "You know I thought he was an alien."

"Who, this Limbaugh being?" said Varcus.

"No. Well, sometimes. But I meant the robot," I said.

"An honest mistake. Although most humanoid types I know don't go prancing around in the buff," said Varcus.

"They do it all the time here, and get paid for it," I said.

"You know, you seem to be obsessed with strippers," said Nicole.

"He brought it up!" I complained.

"Hm. Be that as it may, the robot is quite capable of experiencing everything the same way that you and I do," said Varcus.

"So if he eats a cheeseburger, he's going to be one happy dude?" I said.

"If that's a natural reaction, then yes, he might be," said Varcus.

"It is for me," I said.

The robot entered the room and plopped a thick report onto the table in front of Varcus.

"You ever have a cheeseburger, robot?" I said.

"No, I have not," said the robot.

"Then I guess you're not all that after all," I said.

The robot looked at me, then shook his head and left the room.

"So why are we being evicted, anyway?" I said.

Varcus picked up the report and held it up. It had a green cover, upon which was printed in white letters, *"Planet Earth Environmental Assessment."*

"Because of this," said Varcus. "GREEN's report on the status of the environment of the Earth."

"Who's report?" I said.

"GREEN. Galactic Researchers Encouraging Environmental Niceness," said Varcus.

"Doesn't ring a bell," I said.

"You know; flying saucers. Abductions. Little green men," said Varcus.

"Oh, those guys," said Nicole.

"Yes. They do independent studies of planets, testing for contamination and observing behavioral patterns to determine if a species has become a danger to their own world," said Varcus.

"Is that what's with all the anal probes?" I said.

"No, they're just mean," said Varcus. "But GREEN's report states that you humans have affected the environment of the Earth badly enough that you no longer have the ability and/or willpower to reverse it. Therefore we have no choice but to remove you from the planet before you can do any more damage."

"Can't you just help us fix things?" asked Nicole. "Surely you know what we need to do."

"Yes, but so do all of you," said Varcus. "You're just not doing it. And besides, I'm not allowed to meddle with your place in the environment."

"No, you only decide if we should be allowed to stay in it or be dumped into space," I said.

"Dumped into space? Geebo, I'm not that cruel!" said Varcus. "No, come Monday morning you'll be transported up and moved to another world."

"Does anything good ever happen on a Monday?" I said. "Besides football?"

"So where are you moving us to?" asked Nicole.

"Your new planet is called Gork," said Varcus.

"The name's the first thing that's gonna have to go," I said. "What's it like?"

"Um, it's a bit of a fixer upper, but," said Varcus, hemming and hawing.

"But at least we'll have another home, right?" finished Nicole hopefully. "And we'll be okay there?"

"Well, estimates are that eighty-three percent of you will be dead within the first year, but you could surprise us," said Varcus.

"Glad you're not that cruel," I said.

"You've left us with no choice, I'm afraid. You already have the Earth teetering on the brink of environmental disaster; we can't very well leave you here so you can shove it over the edge," said Varcus.

"I don't suppose you could just go away for a year or two and give us a chance to straighten things up," I said.

"It wouldn't help. Like I said, according to the report you've passed the point where your species can or will put things to right. Believe me, I'm not happy about it either. I've become quite fond of you humans," said Varcus.

"Obviously," I said.

"No, really," said Varcus. "I've spent almost a million years with you people, helping you out, watching over you. And now I have to come here and do this."

"Exactly what do you mean by helping us out?" said Nicole.

"Let me explain," said Varcus. "You see, I'm sort of a case worker for fledgling sentient races. One of my duties is to give them a little assistance whenever they hit a wall in their development. Take Earth for example; I taught your people how to use fire, how to make a wheel, how to fish, how to ride horses."

"Did we figure anything out on our own?" said Nicole.

"Well, you did start hitting each other over the head with rocks without my help," said Varcus brightly.

"Great. Did you teach us about anything cool or fun?" I said.

Varcus thought for a moment. "I did teach you how to make alcohol. You were all getting so tense, fighting and killing one another all the time; I thought it might calm you down a bit. Give you a way to unwind."

"Did it help?" I asked.

"No," said Varcus sadly. "You just killed one another, went home, and got drunk and celebrated. Then you woke up all hung over and grouchy, so you went out and killed each other some more."

"That sounds like us," said Nicole. "So why can't you teach us one more time about the environment?"

"Because, like I said, there's nothing for you to learn; you have all the knowledge you need already," said Varcus.

"I suppose you're right," sighed Nicole. "You know, Varcus, I have to say you look pretty good for someone who's a million years old."

"Thank you, but I'm only one-hundred and twelve," said Varcus. "I didn't hang around while you evolved, if that's what you're asking. I traveled forward through time."

"You can time travel, too?" said Nicole.

"It's not that difficult; anyone can do it. Even you," said Varcus.

"I seriously doubt that," said Nicole.

"No, really; I'll prove it to you. Close your eyes and hold very still, and concentrate hard about something," said Varcus.

"Alright," said Nicole. She closed her eyes and thought very hard about clocks, but got sidetracked by trying to decide between analog and digital.

Varcus sat watching her for a bit, then said, "You see? You just went forward in time thirty seconds."

Nicole opened her eyes. "Very funny."

"It breaks the ice at parties. Anyway, we've just discovered how to go ahead faster. It's going back in time that no one's figured out yet," said Varcus.

"If we're done with the bar tricks can we get back to business before the moving vans arrive?" I said.

"Of course," said Varcus. "But I don't know what else I can tell you; my hands are tied. Planets that can sustain life are a rare and precious thing and it's everyone's duty to protect them, and the Earth is one of the nicer worlds in the galaxy. I'm not sure I would leave you here even if I had the power to do so. As it is, I have to abide by the guidelines set down by the Galactic Council."

"So what am I supposed to do now? Go back and tell everyone there's no hope and they might as well start packing their Samsonites?" I said.

Varcus stood and picked up his PED. "Tell them what I told you; just the facts."

"That should go over big," I said. Nicole and I stood up, and together with Varcus we headed towards the ramp. Varcus tapped on the PED and the door to the outside reappeared and opened. Nicole went through the door then looked back and saw that the walls of the ship were indeed still there from the outside. Curious, she reached out with her hand and felt metal against her fingers, then stuck her head back inside. The walls were still invisible from the interior, but when she tried to put her hand through them found she could not. She came to the conclusion that the walls were like a one way mirror that at the same time somehow let sunlight and air through them.

Varcus and I stood watching Nicole, both of us amused by her experimentation. I waited until she was finished and was about to leave, then remembered something and stopped and turned back to face Varcus. "Oh, by the way; Cynthia said if you mess up her wedding she's going to kick your a-" I began.

"Cynthia?" asked Varcus.

"The gal who owns the farm the computer decided to park you in," I said.

"Oh. Well you can assure her that I've taken every measure not to affect the day to day lives of you humans," said Varcus.

"Like moving us off the planet won't mess up our routines," I said. I started to turn away again, but had yet another thought. "Hey these measures of yours; they wouldn't have anything to do with the fact that we can't get any authority types to come here and help us out, would they?"

"That would be me, yes," said Varcus. "Things go much smoother this way. There's nothing more counter-productive than listening to a room full of bureaucrats argue and point fingers at one another, so I just see to it that they choose to stay away. And that they don't suddenly decide that lobbing a thermonuclear missile or two at me would be a really neat idea."

"And is that why the yard isn't full of reporters and gawkers interviewing bovine witnesses?" I asked.

"That too, yes. Just a little *"nothing to see here, move along"* vibe," said Varcus.

"Must be the same thing Charlie Sheen puts out, but in reverse," I said. "Are you planning on at least eventually letting the rest of the planet in on what's going on, so they can water their plants before they go?"

"Don't worry; everyone will know," said Varcus. "In fact, you might want to catch the broadcast yourself. Just turn on the television tomorrow at noon, your time."

"What channel?" I said.

"All of them," said Varcus. "Everything will be explained."

"Good. And no offense, but I hope everyone leaves you with a big pile of dirty dishes," I said. I put my hand up in goodbye, then exited the spaceship, and the door closed behind me.

Varcus watched us go through the transparent wall, then shook his head sadly and sighed.

"Nice beings; doesn't get much tougher than that," he said somberly, then clapped his hands. "Well, let's see what's on TV."

Chapter Seven

The sun was down, and the birds were all tucked snuggly in their beds. The wedding rehearsal dinner was in full swing in the yard behind the farmhouse, about fifty yards away from, but strategically out of sight of, the alien ship. Two picnic tables were covered with checkered cloths, fried chicken, mashed potatoes, baked beans, and wedding party members and family. I sat at one of the tables with Nicole, Steve and his parents James and Carolyn, and Cynthia and her grandfather Pete. Mark, Craig, Tommy, and the two bridesmaids, Paula and Julia, sat at the other table.

I gnawed hungrily on part of a chicken, having worked up quite an appetite during rehearsal trying to walk down the aisle in a straight line without going too fast or too slow, all the while wondering what the hell to do about the minor fact that we were all well on our way to becoming extra terrestrials.

"Good eats, Cynthia," I said between bites. "You're a lucky man, Steve."

"Yes I am," said Steve, smiling at his fiance.

"You must be lucky too, Jake," said Pete, a kindly looking, elderly gentleman. Pete had the happy and sad duty of standing in at the wedding for Cynthia's parents. "How many people get to meet a real live alien?"

"About ten a month if you believe the Weekly World News," said Nicole.

"You read that rag?" I asked.

"Never," said Nicole, failing to look me in the eye.

"Right," I said.

"So tell us all about this spaceman," said Pete.

"His name is Varcus and-" I began.

"No alien talk during the rehearsal dinner, please!" interrupted Cynthia curtly, evidently still clinging desperately to the hope that she could manage to pull off a normal wedding.

"Now, Cynthia," said Carolyn. "Your grandfather has the right to know what's going on."

"I'm curious myself," said James. "I'd like to know if that ship coming to Earth is going to affect the stock market."

"Oh, yeah; it's gonna affect it alright," I said.

"Do you think I should buy or sell?" asked James.

"I'm guessing it won't make a whole lot of difference either way," I said.

"So is this Varcus fellow more like an ET alien or a Terminator alien?" asked Pete.

"The Terminator was a robot, Granddad," said Cynthia.

"Yeah, but Varcus has one of those, too, and it has almost as bad an attitude as Arnold," I said.

"Why are they here, anyway?" Cynthia asked. "And don't tell me you don't know; I can tell you guys are hiding something."

"They gave you a scroll of some kind, didn't they?" asked Tommy from the next table.

"Yeah, Steve won't talk about it," complained Mark.

"Maybe you will," purred Paula.

"Um," I said. "You know Steve is the one who actually read the scroll; you should probably ask him about it."

"Yeah, but you're the Representative," argued Steve.

"Yeah, but you're the fiance," I countered. "You're the one who's not supposed to be keeping secrets. I'm single; I can be as covert as I want."

"Representative? Representative of what?" asked Carolyn.

"What secrets? What's going on?" asked Pete.

I could tell the crowd was beginning to get ugly, at least as ugly as a wedding party could get, and I looked over at Nicole for help.

"Maybe you should just tell them," said Nicole. "They're going to find out tomorrow anyway."

"You sure that's a good idea?" I said.

"Tell us *what*, Jake?" demanded Cynthia.

Everyone sat staring at me, and I sighed and rubbed my head, which was beginning to lightly throb again. "Okay; if you insist," I said. "Let's see; how can I put this? Cynthia, are you and Steve planning on having kids?"

"Not right this minute," said Cynthia. "So if that's why the spaceship is here you can go tell them we plan to wait, and they can leave and come back later."

"And what do you two plan on using; cloth or disposable?" I asked.

Steve and Cynthia looked at one another, and then back at me. "Are you kidding?" said Cynthia. "Have you ever smelled those things?"

I leaned back on the picnic bench. "The prosecution rests its case."

Cynthia looked at Steve. "That's why the alien is here? Because you and I don't want to wash poopy diapers?"

"Basically, yeah," said Steve.

Cynthia looked at Nicole to see if she too had gone crazy along with we males, but she just shrugged and nodded her head. "I don't get it," said Cynthia.

"Look, the alien says we humans dirtied up the Earth, so he's kicking us off it and moving us to the planet Gork," I said.

"What?!" said Cynthia.

"Gork? What kind of a name is that for a planet?" asked Pete, who had somehow missed the larger problem.

"I doubt if anyone out there in the universe is real impressed with *Earth,* either," I said.

"Can we rename it?" asked Tommy.

"Yes. No. Maybe. I don't know," I said. "The point is, come Monday morning we're scheduled to be evicted."

"Monday?!" screeched Cynthia.

"I'm afraid so," I said.

"They can't move us on Monday!" said Cynthia.

"Would Tuesday be a whole lot better?" I said.

Cynthia pouted. "My honeymoon..." she said sniffily.

"I know how you feel, but-" I said.

"We were going to the Wisconsin Dells!" snapped Cynthia.

"Hey, it could be worse," I said.

"How could it possibly be any worse?" said Cynthia.

"At least you're here with your friends and family," I said. "Imagine the people sitting around the dinner table with Al Gore when he finds out; he's never gonna stop saying I told you so."

Cynthia stood up. "I'm going to go and have a talk with this alien," she said determinedly.

74

I quickly jumped to my feet and moved to intercept. "No, no, no, no. That's not a good idea at all."

"Why not?" said Cynthia.

"Because, Cynthia, you're a great gal who's engaged to my best friend, but you go marching over to that space ship all angry and worked up and Varcus is liable to say *"the heck with this"* and just take off and disintegrate the planet," I said. "And you guys haven't even cut the cake yet."

Cynthia stomped her feet, which had little effect in the soft grass. "What am I supposed to do then?" she asked.

"Go to bed tonight and get up tomorrow and marry that man over there," I said. "Then blame him for the whole thing."

Cynthia sat back down. "Fine. But you keep an eye on that alien."

"Gonna be hard to do tomorrow while I'm making sure you two get hitched," I said.

"Maybe you should just invite him to the wedding, then," suggested Pete.

"Yeah, that's all I need," said Cynthia.

I thought about it for a moment. "You know, that's not a bad idea."

"What?" asked Steve.

"Varcus. Inviting him to your wedding," I said.

"Are you out of your mind?" asked Cynthia.

"Probably," I said. "I do believe I've been talking to aliens and robots lately. Look; this is important, Cynthia. Varcus really needs to come to your wedding."

"No way, Jake. I'm not going to have some little green man getting drunk and eating the DJ," said Cynthia.

"He's purple, not green. Big, too; the DJ would probably only be a light snack for him," I said. "Steve, you know how you're always going on about the planet being doomed? Well here's your chance to try and do something about it."

"I thought the planet was going to be fine once we're gone and it's us who are in trouble," said Steve.

"Picky, picky," I said.

"So how is inviting the alien to my wedding going to help?" said Cynthia.

"No clue," I said. "Maybe give me some time to schmooze him? You guys know how good I am at that. Besides, does anybody here have any better ideas?"

Everyone looked at each other, which made Tommy, Mark, and Craig happy because it gave them all a legitimate excuse to stare at Paula some more.

"Then it's settled; I'll go over there right now and talk to him," I said. "Hey, Steve, why don't you come with me and do the invite?"

"Me? Did you forget already I'm a wuss?" complained Steve.

"Time to man-up," I said. "Come on, it'd be more sincere if you do it. Otherwise he might think I'm just trying to get him out of the ship so we can hit him with something heavy."

Steve got up from the table. "That might not be a bad idea. What about Cynthia?"

Cynthia glared angrily at Steve. "You really want me coming along?" she said through gritted teeth.

"Uh, maybe not," said Steve.

"Yeah, the whole sincerity thing would kinda fly out the window," I said. "Let's go."

Chapter Eight

"You know, you're not getting my marriage off on the right foot, Jake," said Steve, as we approached the ship.

"But someday you can tell the grand kids all about the day the alien danced with their grandmother," I said.

"Our wedding videos are gonna end up on *YouTube*," said Steve.

We walked up the ramp and I knocked on the door. "Hopefully we won't get the butler," I said.

A short moment later the door opened and Varcus stood before us, wearing a long, deep blue puffy robe over silky blue pajamas, his feet nuzzled by fuzzy slippers in the shape of some reptilian alien animal. In his hand was a glass filled with pink glowing liquid, replete with swizzle stick. In the background I could hear the sound of a television.

"Jake! Good to see you again so soon," said Varcus happily.

"I hope we didn't wake you," I said.

"Oh no," said Varcus. "I was just watching some television and unwinding with a nightcap. What can I do for you?"

"I told my man Steve, here, all about you, and he insisted on coming over and meeting you," I said. I looked at Steve, who stood staring at Varcus, and I poked him in the ribs with my elbow. "Isn't that right, Steve?"

"Yes! Yes I did," said Steve. "I was wondering if you'd like to come to my wedding tomorrow," he added quickly, as if to get it out of the way.

"He's marrying Cynthia," I said.

"Really? I'm a bit surprised you'd want me there, all things considered," said Varcus.

"He thought you might be a little lonely out here," I said. "Besides, Steve's one of those save the planet kind of guys too, so he kind of knows where you're coming from."

"Hmm," said Varcus thoughtfully. "This is very unusual. Oh, what the heck; I've never been to an Earth wedding before. It might be fun. I'd be honored to attend."

"Great!" enthused Steve despite probably feeling the exact opposite.

"You know I never asked if you had any friends along in there," I said.

"No, just me and the robot," said Varcus. "Oh, and the thousands of automated transport ships orbiting your planet of course."

"Yeah, can't forget those," I said.

The robot walked up behind Varcus. "You asked me to remind you to change the channel when it's time for *Law and Order*," he said in an annoyed tone.

"I did; switch it for me please," said Varcus.

"Yes, your highnessness," said the robot sarcastically, then moved off to do so.

Varcus sighed. "He gets more surly every day. His model has always been a bit quirky."

"So I noticed," I said. "Would it help if you brought him along tomorrow?"

"Only if I wanted to be miserable. He does need to get out of the ship though; I think he's getting a bit stir crazy," said Varcus.

"Maybe we could find someone to show him around while you're at the wedding," I said.

"That would be most kind of you. And the data he collects could be very valuable. You know, preserving a lost culture," said Varcus.

Steve looked at Varcus with a *"Now why did you have to go and say a thing like that?"* sort of look.

"Oops," said Varcus. "Sorry; don't want to put a damper on things, do we? What time should I be ready?"

"One o'clock okay?" I said. "Or will that get in the way of your broadcast?"

"No, I tend to keep it brief. Most species have such a short attention span these days," said Varcus. "Of course I will miss the Cubs game, but..."

"You like baseball, huh?" I said. "So what do you watch the games on? You got a plasma in there?"

Varcus stepped aside. "See for yourself."

Steve and I stuck our heads into the spaceship and looked; there was now a big, comfortable looking recliner formed out of the floor where our table and chairs had been, and the entire wall was acting as an extremely large, super high-definition TV.

"Wow," I said enviously. "Now that's what I want for the Bears games."

"Packers games," said Steve.

Jake and Steve withdrew their heads from the room. "Whatever," I said. "Guess we'll see you tomorrow then, Varcus."

"I look forward to it," said Varcus. "And thanks again for inviting me."

"No problem. Good night," said Steve.

Varcus waved goodbye and closed the door, and we walked back down the ramp.

"Nice job," I said. "You did pretty well for your first time talking to an alien."

"I just pretended it was a dream without Jessica," said Steve. He looked up at the stars. "I wonder if you can see Gork's sun from here."

"Look for the ugliest ball of gas you can find and that'll probably be it," I said.

81

"They all kind of look alike," said Steve. "But I do see a UFO."

"Ha ha; you said that last night too, and look what happened," I said. "Maybe if you'd stop looking up all the time you'd stop attracting aliens."

"Too late," said Steve.

I put my head back and scanned the night sky, then let my shoulders slump. "Now look what you've done," I said, staring at the brightly lit spacecraft descending towards us. "What is this place, L.A.X. for aliens?"

"We don't have to invite them to my wedding too, do we?" asked Steve nervously.

We watched the new ship glide down towards the Earth. It was elongated, shaped like a classic rocket ship out of the Buck Rogers era, and while it wasn't much larger than Varcus' craft it was certainly a lot gaudier, gold in color and covered with thousands of multicolored lights blinking on and off in eye pleasing patterns. Antennae, radar dishes, and indiscernible apparatuses poked out in every direction from the hull. Moving spotlights shone both into the air and onto the ground as it approached. As it neared the surface, spider-like landing gear unfolded out of bays on the ship's bottom and the vessel glided to a landing about thirty yards or so away from Varcus'. A short ramp with gold posts and velvet ropes for railings unfolded in impressive fashion under a door in the side of the craft, over which unrolled a red carpet. The door slid open and a humanoid stepped out with a flourish, his four hands on his hips, white spotlights shining down on him from the top of the ship.

The new alien could have passed for human if it weren't for his two extra limbs. His facial features were chiseled, handsome in a he-man sort of way, almost like a statue. He stood well over six feet tall, broad shouldered, appearing to be a bit taller due to the pointy gold metal helmet that perched on his head.

He wore a silky red uniform replete with two rows of gold buttons running up and down the front. Each of the hands at the end of his four arms were covered in blue leather looking gloves, while his feet sported matching boots. A wide gold belt wrapped around his waist with several small packs and devices attached to it. A white cape trimmed with gold hung on his bag and rustled in the soft evening breeze. All in all he looked like a cross between Superman and Sergeant Peppers.

"Greetings, people of Earth!" the alien said loudly, his voice booming around the farm. "I bring you good tidings of cheeses and alternative living arrangements. Is there one among you who can speak on your behalf?"

"Not it," I said, and gently pushed Steve towards the alien. "It's your turn to play Representative."

Steve reluctantly walked over to the newcomer. "Hail, citizen!" said the alien in greeting, while snapping off a crisp four handed salute.

"Uh, hail," said Steve, looking down at his own two hands and wondering if and how he was expected to return the salute. "I'm Steve."

"Here is some cheese," said the alien, taking a chunk of a cheese-like substance from one of his packs and handing it to Steve, who looked at it like he'd been handed a live grenade. "Now that I have proven my friendship we can begin negotiations; are you the Representative?"

Steve shook his head no, and pointed over at me.

"Damn!" I said. I sighed and made my way over as Steve happily retreated to Cynthia, who along with the rest of the wedding party had come around the side of the house to find out what all the racket was about. "Jake Williams, Representative; who the hell are you, what do you want, and what did we do now?"

"You sound agitated, citizen," said the alien. "Here, take this cheese and eat it; it will calm you," he said, taking another piece from his pack and trying to hand it to me.

"I'm not taking anything from you," I said. "For all I know that's some sort of dairy based alien lawsuit."

"Hm; you seem suspicious of the cheese. That contradicts my brief studies of the area," said the alien.

"I'm only *visiting* Wisconsin," I said.

"Ah. That would explain the paradox," said the alien. "Then I will try to proceed as best I can. But without the mutual trust that comes with the gift of coagulated animal by-products to an inferior culture, I am dubious of my chances of success."

"We'll just have to muddle along then, won't we?" I said. "Now I'd appreciate it if you'd just tell me who you are and what you want, because we're chock full of aliens right now and I'm not really sure we need another."

"I appreciate your get down to businessness and will do so also," said the alien. "I, am Larry," he said, sticking his enormous chin out as if for emphasis.

"Larry?" I said. "Your name is Larry?"

"Yes. I am glad you are able to understand," said Larry. "I've come to your world to save you and your people."

"An alien named Larry is here to save us?" I said.

"Very good, human," said Larry. "You're much more intelligent than many of your entertainments have led me to believe. Although admittedly the genius of your Rob Schneider cannot be denied."

Varcus, still wearing his robe and fuzzy lizard slippers, hurried over to Larry and I. "Jake, don't listen to a thing that man says; he cannot be trusted."

"Ouch. It hurts my ears to hear you say that, Varcus," said Larry.

"You two know each other?" I said. "I thought this was supposed to be a big universe."

"Not big enough for me to stop bumping into him," said Varcus. "I don't know what harebrained scheme he's cooked up this time, but I beg you not to talk to him."

"Well, if you're going to beg," I said.

"Good. So you'll steer clear of him then?" said Varcus.

"No; at least not yet," I said. "But I do reserve the right to go running and screaming in the opposite direction later."

"Why?" asked Varcus.

"Because I listened to you, didn't I? It's only fair I do the same for Larry here before I start wishing he never landed like I do with you," I said.

"Fine; be that way. I can't stop you. Just please don't sign anything," said Varcus.

"I'll wait until I have an attorney present," I said, then feigned surprise and pointed over at Steve. "Oh look, there's one right over there!"

"Joke if you want; you've been warned," warned Varcus. He turned and headed back to his ship and Larry motioned towards his.

"Perhaps it would be more private if we adjourn to the privacy of my space craft where we might enjoy a modicum of uh, privacy," said Larry.

"Why not? The man says I can't trust you so I'm bound to just walk inside your ship like an idiot," I said. "Lead the way, Larry."

Chapter Nine

The inside of Larry's ship looked like a cheap honeymoon suite. A huge heart shaped bed covered by a red fur spread sat on a raised platform against one bulkhead, under a shining disco ball. A hot tub bubbled by the other side, a Cupid fountain tinkling into it. Furniture was scattered around the room, the couches and chairs covered in crushed velvet and animal print furs. Lava lamps bubbled on every end table, and black velvet paintings that looked like they came from Mexico hung on the walls.

"You know, normally if a strange guy in leather and silk invited me into his bedroom I might be a little leery, but the gay men I know have better taste than this," I said.

"The interior of my ship was scientifically designed to make the fairer and more shoe oriented citizens go weak in the knees upon entering its confines," said Larry.

"And it works, does it?" I asked doubtfully.

"Yes. With the magnitude of my attractiveness I'm not sure it's really necessary, but you can't be too careful when it comes to chicks," said Larry. He took out his PED, showing he too was a member of the growing number of species in the galaxy who couldn't tie their shoes without one, then pressed a button and two paintings swung out of the way to reveal a fully stocked bar. "Martini?"

"Thanks, but I had some drinks in me when I ran into Varcus' robot last night and we all know how that turned out for the Earth," I said.

"Then I'll join you in your abstinence," said Larry. "Please be seated and we'll speak about how I, Larry, will gallantly save your entire race."

Larry and I sat down. "Are you trying to tell me you can stop Varcus from evicting us from the Earth?" I asked, trying to sound hopeful and doubtful at the same time.

"Sorry, that I can't gallantly do," said Larry.

"Then why am I sitting here on a fake zebra fur loveseat?" I said, standing up to leave.

"Because what I can gallantly do is give your people a superior new planet on which to hang their backwards and sideways worn hats," said Larry. "Have you ever been to Gork?"

"Nope, haven't built up enough frequent flier miles yet. But I was in Detroit, once," I said.

"Ah, Detroit. City of muscle cars and flying bullets," said Larry. "I lost one wallet and four watches there one day."

"Yeah, that'd be the one," I said.

"Gork is worse," said Larry.

I sat back down, ready to listen. "Worse, huh? Then you've got my undivided attention," I said. "So what's the deal? Have you got a planet in the Caribbean sector of space that just happens to be vacant?"

"Something similar to that," said Larry. He tapped on his PED and the ship dissolved around us, and he and I and the zebra furniture were suddenly on a beautiful beach covered with alien palm trees.

I surveyed our surroundings as a warm, scented, ocean breeze blew through my hair. The sky above me was rose colored and the water was turquoise, gold specks of light glittering upon it. Two suns, one slightly larger than the other, were just setting on the horizon. Exotic colorful birds flew lazily through the sky. All in all it looked a bit like the British Virgin Islands, but on beauty steroids.

"This is the planet Aurora, home of sandy beaches and rum every night," said Larry. "At least there would be rum if anybody lived there. What do you think?"

"I've seen better," I said, racking my brain for where I could be talking about, as the waves lapped gently against the white sand shore near my feet.

"Sure you have," said Larry.

"If it's so great then why is it empty?" I asked, more than a little skeptical. "You're not trying to run another timeshare scam on me, are you?"

"It's not empty," said Larry. "Many creatures frolic upon its surface, but none of them have bothered to evolve into something that would put up advertising."

"Why hasn't someone colonized it?" I asked.

"You've seen too many of your 2d movies," said Larry. "Real life colonization is most complicated and involves oodles of money and even more oodles of paperwork. Most species don't bother with it and just stay at home."

"So why would it be worth doing for us, then?" I said.

"Because I, Larry, am involved," said Larry.

"That's not an answer," I said. "It sounds more like an impediment, to me."

"Then because it's my planet," said Larry. "And I can do what I want with it."

"How did you end up with your own planet?" I said.

"Lawsuit," said Larry. "I slipped on a Walada peel in a Mega Mart and fell. With gross negligence comes gross settlements."

"Then what's the catch?" I asked.

Larry tapped on the PED and the scene around us disappeared, much to my disappointment.

"There is nothing to catch," said Larry. "You have need of a planet to populate, and I have an empty one that's beginning to gather dust. It would be a most equitable arrangement for both of us."

"But why us in particular?" I said. "I mean, why humans and our inferior culture?"

"You mean, besides the fact you're the only species about to be kicked off their own planet right now?" asked Larry.

"Yes, besides that," I said.

"Pizza," said Larry.

"Pizza?" I said.

"Yes. In spite of your backwardsness your people have created the perfect food," said Larry. "It's round. And tomatoey. And herby. And, and, and..."

"Cheesy?" I said.

"Ah; so you understand cheese after all," said Larry. "Yes, it is cheesy as well. Great, gooey, stringy, golden brown gobs of cheese melting on my tongue and burning the roof of my mouth."

"And that's it? We have pizza so that makes us your immigrants of choice?" I said.

"Could there be a better yardstick by which to measure a specie's worthiness?" asked Larry.

"I guess it'd rate pretty high on who I'd want to co-habitate with, too" I said. "So let me get this straight; we bring the pizza and you move us to this planet of yours. What's it called again? Aldora?"

"Aurora. Like those Northern Lights that I could stare at for hours but don't because they only happen where it's cold," said Larry.

"It's got Gork's name beat by a mile, that's for sure," I said.

"Should I draw up the papers so we can legalize your movement?" said Larry.

"Sure, draw 'em up," I said.

"Most excellent!" said Larry happily.

"But I'm not signing them," I said.

"You're not?" said Larry, not so happily.

"No. At least not yet," I said.

"But why? Either you make the deal and take your pizza to paradise, or you don't and you take it to Gork where it will be most melancholy," said Larry.

I stood up. "Because I never sign anything without talking to my clients first."

"You're going to talk to all the humans?" said Larry. "I must tell you this is a limited time offer. It expires in about one week, not one century."

"I can't talk to everyone, but I can talk to a few people I know," I said. "They'll probably just tell me it's up to me, but at least I'll have asked. Besides, I'd still rather find a way for everyone to stay here on Earth."

Larry stood and put all four of his hands up in front of him in a quadruple *"fine"* sort of gesture. "No problem; I understand. I do not wish to pressurize you.

Take as much of your time as you want. Just don't take any more of it than that."

"I'll get back to you, then" I said. We walked towards the door and stopped at the exit. "So how did you get a planet in a lawsuit? It sounds a wee bit excessive to me for simply falling down."

"I didn't just fall down; I twisted my ankle," said Larry.

"And?" I said.

"It hurt like the dickens," said Larry.

"And they awarded you a planet for that?" I said.

"My people were the only species with lawyers at the time; everyone else had outlawed and/or executed theirs," said Larry. "Since then we've done the same."

"So humans are the only civilized race left in the galaxy with attorneys?" I said.

"No, that would be a contradiction in terms," said Larry. "You cannot use the words lawyer and civilized in a sentence together." He pushed the open button next to the door and it opened, which surprised no one. "Perhaps we could meet and talk some more tomorrow. I would welcome a healthy debate on the merits of pepperoni versus Italian sausage."

"I'm going to be pretty busy; I sort of have a wedding to be in," I said, wondering immediately if it had been a good idea to bring it up.

"A wedding?" said Larry excitedly. "I happen to love weddings as long as I am not the one vowing anything."

"Is that a fact?" I said, sure now it *had* been a bad idea and hoping to just get out of the ship before the conversation finished going where it seemed to be heading.

"Yes. There are always females there, full of desire to find a mate after watching a member of their chromosome club become legally attached," said Larry. He looked at me with an attempt at puppy dog eyes, which in a roundabout way worked because it creeped me out so bad I would've done anything to make him stop.

"I know Cynthia's gonna kill me for this, but we already invited your neighbor alien to the wedding so I guess I should invite you too," I said.

"Why, thank you. You certainly didn't need to do that," said Larry, feigning surprise.

"I really didn't want to see you start crying, either," I said. "Be ready at one o'clock and meet up with Varcus; you two can go together. That should annoy him."

"Yes, it will, I guarantee," said Larry.

I waved goodbye and exited the ship, then walked over towards Steve and the rest of the wedding party, who were slowly heading towards the house, bored already with the new alien.

"So is he coming to my wedding?" said Steve.

"You know he is," I said.

"Great. And are you going to tell Cynthia?" said Steve.

"No, you are, but she'll blame me like always," I said.

"That seems fair," said Steve. "You coming inside?"

I looked over at Nicole, who was standing off by herself taking pictures of Larry's ship. I decided I could use a little normalcy, like talking to a pretty woman. "Yeah, in just a minute."

Steve went inside the house and I walked over to Nicole. "So who's the new guy?" she asked.

"Just some real estate agent. He has some beach front property he thought we might be interested in opening a pizza parlor on; I told him we'd think about it," I said.

"If you say so," said Nicole. "You know I'd love to see the inside of his ship, too."

"Just don't go without a chaperone; with those four arms of his I don't think you'd make it out of that love pit unmolested," I said.

"Thanks for the warning." Nicole took one last picture and put her camera in her shirt pocket. "So what are you going to do now?" she asked.

"Probably go inside and get some sleep. You?" I said.

"I guess I'll head back over to the bed and breakfast. I hate to though. I don't know what I might miss," said Nicole.

"You could stay with me," I said.

Nicole looked at me in surprise.

"With us!" I said quickly. Although now that I'd accidentally said what I'd said I knew I'd meant it, and instantly wished I could retract my retraction. "Us meaning everyone in there. Not with me, me, but in the farmhouse I mean. Although I'd be in there too. You know, just not..."

Nicole was still studying me quizzically, so I continued my clarification.

"Plenty of space; lots of bedrooms; big house," I said.

"That's what I thought you meant," said Nicole.

"Uh-huh," I said.

We stood awkwardly silent for a moment, looking everywhere but at one another. I felt like a rank amateur; I was much suaver while actually *trying* to pick up a girl than I was when I found myself accidentally doing so.

"What?!" yelled Cynthia angrily from inside the house, breaking the silence nicely. "Steve…"

"What was that all about?" asked Nicole, startled.

"That would be all about me," I said. "Come on, we better get inside before Steve ends up with a black eye for the wedding pictures."

Chapter Ten

"Yeah, ma, I know. I'm doing everything I can," I said into my cell phone. "No, I don't know what the weather is like on Gork this time of year. I know it makes packing difficult but I don't know if we get to bring anything anyway. No, I don't think we're all going to be running around naked. Just watch the broadcast. And let dad have a drink if he wants one. In fact, let him have two. Look, ma, I gotta go. Yes, I'll be sure and tell the alien that. Bye mom. Love you, too. Bye. Bye." I hung up the phone and put it in my tux pocket.

"What are you supposed to tell Varcus?" asked Steve, as he paced nervously back and forth in the waiting room of the church.

"My dad needs a firm mattress," I said.

"Hey, do you think this is it?" asked Craig, pointing at the TV.

Steve, Mark, and I gathered around the television. The screen was black, except for some green letters that said *"A message to all Earthlings."*

"Yeah, this might be it; nice job figuring that out, Craig," said Steve condescendingly.

"Thanks," said Craig.

The TV screen changed, and showed Varcus sitting at a table in the room on his ship where he'd met with us, wearing a shiny blue suit in the style of his planet, with a white vest and light blue ascot. He stared blankly at the camera, smiling. "Is this thing on?" he said finally. "Are we live? Okay. Hello, people of Earth! My name is Varcus Gromell, and I come from the planet Vandor. Recently the Galactic Council received a report-" Varcus stopped and looked around him, then addressed someone off camera. "Robot! Where is the report? I thought I told you to have it here on the table for the broadcast! Yes, I can see it's not here. Where is it? Never mind, it's too late now; we'll talk about it later." He turned back to the camera. "Well, I have it here somewhere. Anyway, it's from the independent environmental testing organization GREEN, and simply put, their conclusion is that you humans have pushed the Earth to the brink of environmental disaster to the point where you no longer have the knowledge and desire to reverse what you have done. Therefore, to protect the planet from any further harm, you are to be evicted from it on Monday morning, nine AM, U.S. Central Time."

"So it's true," said Mark. "I thought maybe you guys were pulling some elaborate practical joke."

"We still could be," said Steve.

"Not anymore. It's on TV, so it must be true," said Craig.

"Spoken like a true American," I said.

Varcus continued. "You will all be, in your Earth cultural terms, beamed up to one of thousands of transport ships now in orbit around your planet, then relocated to your new home on the planet Gork in the Keeselhorse System. You may bring with you only what you can carry. Weapons and explosives are not allowed, although since there is a soothing pacifist ray currently aimed at your planet you wouldn't think to bring them anyway. But I thought I'd mention it just in case."

"Good thing it's not football season right now," I said. "They'd probably have to play touch."

"I heard on the news that the crime rate over the last couple of days was at a new all time low," said Mark. "Zero. All the wars have come to a screeching halt, too."

"Something good came out of all this, anyway," said Steve.

"Also, you will not be allowed to bring live animals," said Varcus. "Your pets will be well taken care of after you depart, and we wouldn't want to destroy the eco system on Gork, such as it is, with a stray gerbil or goldfish, now would we? The seven or so billion of you should be quite enough of a shock to the poor planet. A short film will follow this announcement giving you all the information you'll need to prepare for the move to your new home. It should be noted that for the first thirty days of your life on Gork there will also be a pacifist ray pointed at *that* planet, so you'll have to wait before you can begin to throw rocks and spears at one other. That's about it from me; it's been nice talking to you. Enjoy the film, and have a great and happy Earth day!"

Varcus sat smiling for a long moment. "Okay, you can hit the button now," he said, from the corner of his mouth.

Nothing happened, and he remained grinning stupidly at the camera as seconds ticked by. Finally he said, "Look, you half-witted robot, just start the drooging film before I-"

The picture on the TV went blank, then switched to a cheesy screen that read, "*You and your big move to Gork!*" Equally cheesy music soon began, as did a low budget cartoon, featuring a human standing in the middle of his living room, scratching his head as a voice over began.

"*So you and your people are moving to Gork,*" said the narrator. "*How exciting for you! You probably have many questions, and I'm here to help. Let's ask Sam, a typical human being, what he thinks he might need to know.*"

"You've got to be kidding me," I said.

The cartoon Sam looked at the camera. "I guess first I'd like to know what the heck I should I bring with me!"

"*That's entirely up to you, Sam!*" said the narrator happily. "*You could bring your golf clubs, blender, pink flamingo, teddy bear, grandfather clock, Rice Krispy bars, CD collection, chainsaw, why even the kitchen sink!*" he said, the cartoon film piling all the items onto Sam as it spoke. *"But keep in mind there's no electricity on Gork at the moment, so you may just want to bring some clothes and a good book; and maybe that teddy bear."*

"I would like to bring some clothes," said Sam. "But what's the weather like on Gork?"

"If you live in a warm climate you're going to like it on Gork!" said the narrator, enthusiastically. *"And if you live in a cold one, you'll never have to worry about those freezing winters again! The average temperature on Gork is a balmy one-hundred and twelve degrees Fahrenheit!"*

"Gee, it sounds better than a day at the beach!" said Sam excitedly.

"Okay; Sam's an idiot," said Steve.

"They did say he was a typical human," I said.

"When you arrive on Gork you'll find temporary shelters, water, and enough rations to last six Gorkian months, so you'll have everything you'll need to get started!" said the narrator. *"But don't forget, one day on Gork is only about nine Earth hours long, so you'll have to get busy finding those alternative food sources in a hurry. Just think how short your work day will be!"*

"That sounds great! Can I go right now?" said Sam.

The cheesy music swelled to a happy conclusion as the film wound down.

"Be patient, Sam; the big day will come soon enough," said the narrator. *"We hope the rest of you humans are now as*

excited as Sam about your big move to the planet Gork. We look forward to watching you scratch and claw to tame this wild and vibrant planet. Thanks for watching, and have a great and happy Earth day!"

The screen went blank, then switched back to regular Earth programming.

"I don't know about the rest of you, but somehow I don't feel a whole lot better," said Steve.

"Yeah, I'd say a general state of panic would have set in just now if it wasn't for that ray," I said. "By the way, Steve, did you ever find anyone to baby sit Varcus' toaster?"

"Yeah, but it wasn't easy," said Steve. "Most of the people I know are either going to be at the wedding or for some reason had no desire to hang out all day with a grumpy alien robot."

"But you did get someone, didn't you?" I said.

"Yes. Actually he kind of jumped at the chance," said Steve. "I had to give him some money to entertain the robot with, but at least he's doing it."

"Really? Who'd be crazy enough to actually *want* to do it?" I asked.

A knock sounded on the door of Varcus' ship, and he walked over and pressed a button and the door slid open. Outside stood a young man with long hair wearing a pair of ratty jeans, a sleeveless Metallica T-shirt, and a red bandanna. He held up his hand, his thumb index and pinky fingers extended.

"Ola, alien dude!" said Johnny.

Chapter Eleven

Varcus and Larry entered the back of the small Lutheran church, Varcus still wearing his blue suit from the broadcast. Larry was dressed in a tight white leather uniform trimmed in gold that made little crunching sounds as he walked. The organist noticed the pair and hit a bad note and stopped playing, and before long a wave of whispers and head turns occurred until the church fell dead silent and everyone sat staring at them. Varcus and Larry looked around and smiled at all the faces as Tommy the usher approached.

"Are you on the bride's side or the groom's?" asked Tommy nervously.

Varcus looked confused, then leaned down and spoke quietly to Tommy. "You mean humans even pick sides at a wedding? No wonder you fight all the time," he said.

"Do you have special seating for celebrities?" asked Larry hopefully.

"Uh, I just need to know if you're friends with the bride or groom," said Tommy, who hadn't asked for any of this.

"Oh. Well I have nothing against Cynthia, but given the fact she's made threats against my person perhaps we should sit in the groom's section," said Varcus.

Tommy glanced around, then walked Varcus and Larry down the aisle as everyone stared. Varcus greeted people with a nod of the head or hello, while Larry strutted and waved as if he were in a parade. When they got to the fourth row from the front Tommy motioned for them to sit and people slid down to make room, crunching together to give the aliens a wide berth. Larry sat down and Varcus squeezed in, looking a little squished, as the organist resumed playing and the guests started talking again in quiet whispers.

Varcus looked around at the beautiful little church. Lavender and blue flowers and ribbons decorated the interior. Pastor Dave, a kindly looking gray-haired man in his late fifties, stood wearing his robes by the dais at the front of the room. People talked amongst themselves, some about the aliens, but many about the wedding.

Varcus leaned over towards Larry. "You know, there is quite the air of anticipation."

"I'm sure it helps to have two stylish aliens in attendance," said Larry. "Well, one, anyway."

"Oh, yes; as if wearing skin tight leather to the wedding was stylish, not to mention appropriate," snapped Varcus.

"At least I'm wearing wedding white and don't blend in with the decorations," argued Larry.

"I don't blend in," said Varcus huffily.

"You're right, you don't. You stick out like a handful of sore thumbs," said Larry.

"See here you little-" began Varcus rather loudly, before several people in the vicinity shushed him. The two sat quietly for a moment, then Varcus said, "Look; seeing as how we're stuck with one another I suggest we put aside our differences for the time being and try to get along."

"Agreed. Getting thrown out of the wedding would do little to bolster either of our reputations here on Earth," said Larry.

"Good," said Varcus. The two shook hands and sat back in the pew. "I'm quite looking forward to this; it should be an interesting experience. And I have to remember to thank Johnny for getting the robot out of my hair for a while."

"Who?" asked Larry, checking out a blonde in the third row.

"The nice young man entertaining my DA-42," explained Varcus. "He seemed very eager to help, and that's a rare thing in the universe these days. I think he'll be a very good influence on the robot."

"Explain this to me again," said the robot, while sitting on a bar stool in the Moosehead Tavern. "Why am I licking my hand?"

"Ya gotta wet it, dude," said Johnny. "Otherwise the salts gonna fall off."

"And why exactly do I want salt sticking to me?" asked the robot.

"So you can lick it off," said Johnny.

"I'm putting it on so I can lick it back off?" said the robot.

"Yeah, man," said Johnny.

The robot thought about this. "So basically I could put it anywhere I want as long as it sticks?"

"If that's your thing," said Johnny.

"Fine," said the robot. He leaned down and licked the bar, then poured salt on it and sat back to look, satisfied with the results. "There."

Johnny shook his head and laughed. "You're one crazy dude, dude. We're gonna get along great."

The robot eyed Johnny suspiciously with his little black eyes. "We are?" he said.

"Yep," said Johnny, then he stuck out his tongue and gave the bar a good wet smear before pouring salt on it. He then picked up his shot glass with one hand and his lime wedge with the other, the robot watching and carefully and mimicking him. "To us! Two crazy dudes!" said Johnny.

The robot examined Johnny and cocked his head to one side quizzically, then looked pleased at finding someone who actually seemed to like him for a change.

Johnny licked the salt off the bar, drank down the tequila, and bit into the lime before grimacing. The robot watched and did the same, but without the grimace.

"Hmm. Interesting," said the robot.

"What?" said Johnny.

"An intense burning sensation in my throat, followed by an overwhelming impulse to gag," said the robot. "Then a weird but not altogether unpleasant feeling in my head."

"That's tequila alright. You want another?" asked Johnny.

"Tequila. Yes, I think I should try that again," agreed the robot. "For data."

Johnny looked down at the bartender and held up two fingers, and pointed at the bar in front of him. "You mean the robot guy on Star Trek?"

"Who?" said the robot.

"Dude, you need to get out more," said Johnny.

The bartender poured the shots and served them along with two more lime wedges, and Johnny and the robot licked the bar and poured salt on their respective puddles.

"To Data!" said Johnny, toasting the fictional android.

"To data!" said the robot, toasting non-fictional bits of information.

They licked the salt off the bar again, taking with it another herd of innocent germs that had been living there peacefully, who were quickly annihilated by a wave of Cuervo.

Steve stood at the altar in the front of the church near Pastor Dave. The organist began to play *"Canon in D,"* and all heads turned to watch as Mark came down the aisle accompanying Julia in her lavender bridesmaid's dress, followed quickly by Craig and Paula. I came next, walking arm and arm with Nicole while trying not to think about all the things I was thinking about.

There was a pause and the music changed to *"The Bridal Chorus."* Cynthia in white came slowly down the aisle accompanied by Pete. I took a moment to glance over at the aliens to see what they were up to, to make sure they weren't about to do something that would get them *and me* into severe amounts of trouble with the bride. Varcus sat smiling ear to ear as Cynthia went past, obviously quite taken by the event transpiring around him, while Larry appeared to be busy examining the bridesmaids.

Cynthia didn't seem to notice either of them, too caught up in her day to be distracted by any purple or four armed aliens. When they got to the front she kissed Pete on the cheek, and he sat down in the left front pew, while Cynthia took her place next to a happy looking Steve.

"Good afternoon," said Pastor Dave. "We are gathered to celebrate the marriage of Steve Anderson and Cynthia Larson. They have come here today because of the love they feel for one another, and ask you to witness and share in their commitment as they embark on their journey together. A journey of hope that looks ahead to their new future as one."

Varcus leaned over and spoke quietly to Larry. "This is so exciting!" said Varcus "Perhaps I should have brought the robot; he could have used some Earth culture to settle him down."

"Who knows? Maybe he's getting some Earth culture right now," said Larry.

The opening guitar riffs of *"Sweet Child of Mine"* rang out loudly through the bar, and the robot jumped off his barstool and covered his ears. "Aggh! What is that?" he said, wondering if this was some sort of auditory weapon the humans had secretly developed.

"A classic, man," said Johnny.

"Yes, but what is it?" asked the robot.

"Rock and roll, dude. Haven't you ever heard rock and roll before?" asked Johnny.

"Apparently not, as I am still able to hear," said the robot.

"Dude! If we're gonna be buds you gotta learn to rock. This is Axel and Slash, man; G 'n R!" said Johnny.

"Okay; just warn me the next time we are about to rock," said the robot. "My audio circuits almost overloaded. I've lowered my volume now."

"Just so you have it up loud; it's got to be loud," said Johnny.

"It is loud; I can barely hear you," said the robot, and he sat back down on his bar stool.

"Cool. Bartender! Dos margaritas, por favor," said Johnny.

"What is a margarita?" said the robot.

"You'll like it; it has tequila," said Johnny.

"Good," said the robot.

Johnny leaned back and bit his lower lip and played air guitar, bobbing his head in rhythm to the music. The robot watched him, then slowly began to do the same in mechanical fashion.

"Sweet, dude!" said Johnny. "Now you're rockin' Earth style!"

"Do you, Cynthia, take Steven Roger Anderson to be your lawfully wedded husband, to love and care for him, in sickness and in health, till death do you part?" said Pastor Dave.

"I do," said Cynthia.

"And do you, Steven, take Cynthia Patricia Larson to be your lawfully wedded wife, to love and care for her, in sickness and in health, till death do you part?" said Pastor Dave.

"I do," said Steve.

I looked over at Nicole and she looked back at me and smiled, as Steve and Cynthia exchanged rings.

"Friends and family, I present to you all; Steve and Cynthia Anderson, husband and wife," said Pastor Dave. "You may kiss the bride."

Steve laid a good long kiss on Cynthia, as the people in the pews stood and applauded. The wedding party made a two at a time exit out of the back of the church, and I snuck in a quick wave to the interstellar duo as I waltzed past.

Varcus took a silk handkerchief out of his pocket and dabbed at a tear in his eye. "That was quite moving. I guess I got carried away in the moment."

"My own manliness keeps me from performing such public displays" said Larry. "That's why I will only watch *Rudy* in the privacy of my ship."

"That one gets me every time, too," said Varcus. "What happens now, I wonder?"

"If I know my weddings it's party time!" said Larry.

Chapter Twelve

Varcus and Larry stood near the end of a long line going into the main room of the VFW. Varcus craned his neck to look around the people to try and see what was going on up front, then Larry did the same. Varcus did this once again, then looked irritated and turned to Larry. "I thought you said it was party time," he said.

"It should be; perhaps this is some slow moving form of line dancing I am not familiar with," said Larry. He tapped a teenage boy in front of him on the shoulder. "Excuse me, adolescent citizen. Could you tell me at what point this wedding business is going to become fun? We thought there were going to be festivities."

"There are. This is just the receiving line," said the boy.

"Ah," said Varcus. "So we're in line for our food and drink?"

"No," said the boy snottily.

"Then what exactly is it we're doing here? Besides showing off our queuing skills," said Larry. "I saw chicks; where are they?"

"Look; it's hard to explain," said the boy. "The bride and groom and their parents are at the front of the line waiting to greet everyone."

Larry peered around the long line again. "Well can't they just wait until everyone's inside and greet us all at once?"

"That's not how it's done. We each talk to them personally," said the boy.

"I see. What are we supposed to say?" said Varcus.

"Most people say the same kind of thing; congratulations. You must be very proud. It was a lovely wedding," explained the boy.

"Seems like an awful lot of standing around just to say something everyone knows you're going to say anyway," said Larry grumpily.

"Then say something else," said the teen.

"Like what?" said Varcus.

"How should I know? Be original. You're the ones from another planet," said the boy.

"You know, on Tweellar Two it is customary to serve the groom's father as the main course at the celebration dinner," said Larry, as he shook James' hand.

"That's...interesting," said James, looking a bit worried.

Larry nudged James in the ribs and winked. "Lucky for you we're on Earth, eh? At least for the moment," he said, then moved on to Carolyn. "And on

Udal Major the groom's mother is ceremoniously dipped in Penoli oil then-"

Varcus quickly intervened and grabbed Larry by one of his arms and pulled him away. "Sorry; he's not from around here," he said.

"Yes, I'd guessed that," said Carolyn.

Varcus turned, and found Cynthia next in line. "Ah, Cynthia," he said warmly. "We meet at last. I just wanted to say that-"

Cynthia interrupted him. "And I just wanted to say that you better hope this wedding turns out to be like a fairy tale I'm going to remember for the rest of my life, no matter how short it turns out to be on this Gork place of yours, or so help me you're going to be the sorriest alien who ever landed in my pasture. Got it, Mr. Martian?"

"Yes, ma'am," said Varcus quietly, edging away from Cynthia. He quickly shook Steve's hand, then backed away.

"Would it help your wedding's fairy-taleness if I performed an alien abduction and stole the bride?" asked Larry. "I have a hot tub and champagne and an extensive Michael Bolton collection and we could..." he said, trailing off under Cynthia's withering glare. "Maybe next time."

The alien pair moved off away from the line. "I think that went well," said Larry.

117

"Oh very nice," said Varcus. "I'm sure hinting at eating the groom's parents is a big hit at Earth weddings." He looked around the small crowded reception hall. "This way."

"Where are we going?" said Larry.

"To the bar," said Varcus. "Come on, I need a drink."

"So this Farcon guy," said Johnny, drunkenly. "He doesn't respect you much, does he?"

"No, he doesn't," slurred the robot back, as he wobbled on his bar stool. "Always telling me what to do. Never asks me what I want to do. What my needs are."

"And you don't even have a name?" said Johnny.

"Nope. He just calls me robot," said the robot.

"Wow, dude," said Johnny.

"Yeah, dude," agreed the robot.

"That'd be like my mom calling me human," said Johnny, taking a gulp from his margarita. He thought about it. "Although I guess that would be better than most of the stuff she calls me."

"Duuuude," said the robot, liking the word more and more. He took the umbrella out of his drink and stuck it behind his left ear, giving him a match to the one behind his right.

"You know what I'm going to do?" asked Johnny.

"Order more margaritas?" suggested the robot hopefully.

"No," said Johnny. "Well yes, but after that. I'm gonna give you a name."

"You are?" said the robot.

"I am. And then we'll have those cheeseburgers," said Johnny.

"So I can tell the Representative I am all that after all," said the robot.

"Right. Then we're going skateboarding," said Johnny.

The robot managed a dismount from his bar stool, and stood up unsteadily. "Okay, but first I have to go to the can again." He said, then giggled. "The can; I love that."

"Dude, you just went a couple minutes ago!" said Johnny.

"I know. They must have outfitted me with a teensy-weensy synthetic bladder," said the robot.

"Maybe you can get an upgrade," said Johnny.

"I'll talk to Ficus about that too," said the robot. He took one step towards the bathroom and fell flat on his face with a loud clatter. "And maybe an upgrade for my feet," he said, while pushing himself up off the dirty floor.

Johnny looked him up and down. "Hey, how do you..." he said, motioning his head towards the bathroom.

"Oh. Would you like to come in and watch?" asked the robot.

"Duuude! You never ask another dude into the bathroom with you; only chicks do that," said Johnny.

The robot shrugged. "Okay," he said, and staggered off towards the bathrooms.

"And go in the right one this time!" Johnny shouted after him. He turned back to the bar and picked up his margarita, just as the sound of girls screaming came from the direction of the bathrooms. "Too late."

Chapter Thirteen

The wedding had moved into the wind down phase, a smattering of guests still scattered around the ballroom. I sat at a large, round table near the dance floor with Nicole, Steve and Paula. We were all watching Varcus, who was up at the DJ and karaoke setup, microphone in hand, doing a passable version of *"Old Time Rock and Roll"* while Larry danced wildly about on the dance floor, bouncing from one woman to the next.

"Don't you people ever do anything without Karaoke?" I asked.

"Not really, no," said Steve, as Cynthia came back from her latest mingle and plopped down on his lap.

It'd been an interesting affair, to say the least. While Varcus hadn't consumed anyone and Larry had been on his best behavior, other than hitting on and dancing with just about every woman in the VFW, it certainly wasn't your typical wedding. Even something as traditional as the Hokey Pokey had taken on a whole new twist when Varcus had joined in, and Larry and his strangely compelling Rubber Chicken Dance had been downright bizarre.

"So this is the guy that's tossing us off the Earth," said Cynthia, who was having a difficult time disliking Varcus no matter how hard she tried. Despite being an alien from another planet he had a down to

121

Earth quality and had gotten along famously with everyone in attendance, especially the children, who had followed him around like the Pied Piper.

"Weird huh? He's more like the crazy uncle that gets drunk and falls in the wedding cake," I said, as Nicole snapped yet another picture of the aliens.

Paula ran her finger around the rim of her champagne glass. "I think he's kind of sexy. I wonder how he-"

"You're not sleeping with the alien," said Cynthia.

"Why not?" pouted Paula. "It is a wedding."

"Yes, it's a wedding; not a science experiment," said Cynthia.

"But we are trying to find a way to get him to call off the eviction," I pointed out. "Maybe if she-"

"Forget it," said Cynthia.

"Party pooper," said Paula.

"He's sure been having a good time," said Steve.

"He sure has," I said, then turned to Nicole. "Do you think any of this is helping?"

"I don't know, but I guess it can't hurt," said Nicole.

"It can hurt my wallet. I'm almost out of cash from buying the two of them drinks," I said.

"Maybe if Varcus gets to know some humans he might be reluctant to move us," said Nicole.

"That's what I was hoping for, but we'll see," I said.

Cynthia got up off of Steve's lap again and held out her hand to him. "Come on, Stevie. It's time for you to go home and spend some quality time with your new bride."

"Yes, ma'am. That I can do," said Steve, taking Cynthia's hand and standing up.

"Don't do anything I wouldn't do," I said.

"You mean like get married? Too late," said Steve. He and Cynthia left arm in arm as Varcus wrapped up his song. He took a bow as Larry approached the stage.

"Go sit your vocal chords down before they do any more damage," said Larry. "Let a rabid viewer of *American Idol* show you how it's done."

Varcus looked annoyed but got off the stage and went over to our table and sat down, his clothes a bit disheveled from hours of exuberant fun. He picked up a champagne glass and finished its contents and said "This karaoke is most enjoyable. I must say you humans really know how to throw a party."

"Some species don't?" I asked.

"Most species don't. They're all too busy being civilized," said Varcus.

"Guess us barbarians have something to offer after all," I said.

"No argument there," said Varcus.

The music started and Larry began to sing *"I'm Too Sexy,"* gyrating all over the small riser as the last of the female guests gathered under the stage and cheered him on.

"Now that's something I really didn't need to see," I said.

"Oh, I don't know," purred Paula, and she stood up and sashayed towards the stage.

Varcus' PED beeped at him and he took it out and checked it, looking puzzled and concerned.

"Is something wrong?" asked Nicole.

"It's a message from the robot," said Varcus.

"What does it say?" I said.

"I'm not sure," said Varcus, staring blankly at the small screen. "It's long and rambling with a lot of exclamation points. It seems to be a series of references to shoving several of my appendages into a variety of my orifices."

"Can I see it?" I said.

Varcus gave the PED to me, and at that moment I probably had the power in my hands to not only save the human race, but to cure cancer, end hunger, and finally win the Cubs a World Series.

"Wow," I said, in reference to the message and not all my newly acquired abilities.

"Do you know what he's babbling about?" asked Varcus.

"Yes, but I think you better talk to him about it," I said. "I try not to get involved in family disputes without a retainer." I handed the PED back to Varcus, and the Cubs lost yet another opportunity.

"He may be malfunctioning; I better get back to the ship," said Varcus, standing up to leave.

"Wait, I'll come with you," I said, standing up as well. "You coming, Nicole?"

"You two go ahead," said Nicole. "I better stay and keep an eye on Paula."

I looked over at the stage, which Paula had planted herself in front of, dancing sexily for an obviously interested Larry. "Good luck with that; you'll need it," I said, then headed towards the door with Varcus.

Chapter Fourteen

The robot hummed the chorus of *"Highway To Hell,"* and leaned back unsteadily to admire his work. He was in a surprisingly good mood, surprising in that he had never been in a good mood before. He wished he had a mirror so he could look at himself again and see the blue bandana on his head, the holey jeans covering his spindly legs, the beat up Converse All Stars squeezed onto his feet, and his already beloved Guns N' Roses Tee shirt. His new wardrobe had been a gift from Johnny, who wasn't around right now, having left the robot alone to go searching for something called Twinkies.

The robot smiled a drunken smile as he thought about his new, only, and first friend, then shook the paint can and started spraying the last "s" in *"Varcus sucks"* on the brick wall of the feed store. He finished it and was contemplating the aesthetic value of adding an exclamation point, when red and blue flashing lights lit the area, and he turned and put up his hands in surrender.

"Busted!" he said.

Chapter Fifteen

"Well, he's not in there," said Varcus, emerging from the ship.

"I'm sure he'll turn up," I said, standing at the top of the ramp. "Not many places he can hide, unless he gets a job as a crash test dummy."

Just then the sheriff's car pulled up into the driveway and over to the fence in the yard. Sheriff Johnson and Deputy Roberts got out and opened the back door and helped the robot out, still wearing his new old clothes, and supported him across the pasture over to the bottom of the ramp.

"I think this belongs to you," said the sheriff.

"I'm afraid so," confirmed Varcus.

"He! He belongs to you, not this belongs to you," protested the robot drunkenly. "Except I don't belong to him. I've just been letting let him boss me around because I haven't had anything better to do."

The sheriff and deputy let go of the robot, and he stood uncertainly for a moment before falling to the ground in a heap.

"I'm very sorry, officers," said Varcus apologetically.

"No worse than picking up my cousin Roy every Saturday night," said the sheriff.

Roy stuck his head out the back window of the sheriff's car. Can we get going soon? It's almost time for me to puke."

"See what I mean? Good night," said Sheriff Johnson.

"Good night. And thank you, officers," said Varcus.

The sheriff and deputy got in the car and drove away, Roy waving out the window at the robot as they went. "Bye, little buddy! And don't forget to tell your boss I think he's a horses a-" said Roy, a couple of s's lost as the sheriff rolled up the back window.

I looked down the ramp at the robot lying face down in the grass. "Oops; looks like someone had a good time."

"Robot! Pick yourself up and get up here!" demanded Varcus.

The robot tried to push himself to his feet but couldn't muster it, so instead slowly crawled up the ramp, metal hands scraping against its surface. When he finally got to the top Varcus glared down at him, hands on his hips.

"Alright, robot, what do you have to say for yourself?" said Varcus.

"My name isn't robot," said the robot, totally inebriated. "It's Robb. Robb Ott."

"What on Kelgrin are you talking about?" asked Varcus.

"Dude. My name. It's Robb Ott. (Hic). Get used to it," said Robb.

"We'll see about that," said Varcus. "Turn off your simulation circuits immediately and get inside!"

"No," said Robb.

"No? What do you mean no?" said Varcus irritably.

"No, as in no," said Robb. "I like being drunk and miserable; it feels good for some reason. I think I'm going to just wallow in it for a while."

"You sure that's a good idea?" I asked. "You know if you really do simulate humans..."

Robb made a gurgling sound, and margaritas, cheeseburgers, and Slim Jims suddenly tsunamied across the ramp towards my rented shoes.

"That's what I was afraid of," I said, picking up my feet. "Man, that's just nasty."

"Sorry, Jake," said Varcus.

"You got a mop in there?" I said.

"Don't worry about it. After you leave I'll turn on the frictionless surface and it'll just slide right down the ramp," said Varcus. "You happy now, robot?"

Robb didn't answer and instead began mumbling random lines from *"For Those About to Rock"* as he put his hand up in the air, pinky, thumb, and index finger extended.

"I guess that means yes," I said. "So, Varcus; did *you* have a good time at the wedding tonight, too?"

"I certainly did, Jake. Very much so," said Varcus.

"And did you like all the people you met?" I asked.

"Oh, yes. They were all quite warm and kind; especially the children," said Varcus.

"So does this mean we can forget all about this whole, silly, eviction thing?" I said hopefully.

Varcus paused and looked at me. "No," he said. "But I did have a good time," he added brightly.

"Swell. Glad to hear it," I said sulkily.

"Don't let the man get you down, Jake! (Hic)," said Robb.

"You be quiet," said Varcus.

"Monday morning we're going to get yanked out of here and brought to someplace that's going to make us all wish we could live together in Siberia instead, and there's not a thing we can do about it," I said. "So yeah, the man's going to get me down."

"Damn the man!" said Robb, thrusting his fist into the air.

"Thanks for the moral support, Robb," I said.

"No problemo," said Robb. "You know, dude, you could always ask for a hearing."

"A what?" I said.

"Robot..." warned Varcus.

"A hearing. It's your right as Representative. The man here probably didn't think it was worth mentioning," said Robb. "Damn the man!"

"Varcus? Is that true? Is there some sort of legal way I can fight the eviction?" I said.

"Well, technically, yes," said Varcus.

"Technically?" I said. "What does that mean?"

"It means that yes, you have the right to a hearing, but it's pointless. There's no way to fight the facts of GREEN's report, Jake," said Varcus.

"Well, I want one anyway," I said.

"Why? It would just be a waste of time. And it would mean I'd have to postpone the eviction for another day," said Varcus.

"Boy, that would be a shame now, wouldn't it?" I said.

"Yes, it would," said Varcus.

"I like you, Varcus," I said. "I really do. But I like my planet more."

"If you liked your planet so much you'd let me do what's best for it and take you all off of it in a timely fashion," said Varcus.

"Then let me rephrase; I like *being on* my planet more. I want my hearing," I said.

"That's tellin' him, Jake! (Hic)," said Robb. "Damn the man!"

"Thanks, but I think that's enough damning for now," I said. "So, Varcus?"

Varcus sighed. "Very well. As I said, it is your right. We'll leave tomorrow morning, then."

"Leave?" I said.

"We can't very well do it here, can we?" said Varcus.

"I don't know. I guess I don't know how all this works," I said. "Where are we going?"

"To Kador, the galactic capital," said Varcus.

"As in, another planet Kador?" I said.

"Do you know of another one?" said Varcus.

"No, but I've got an atlas in my Humvee," I said. "I'd be glad to check."

"You'll be going in front of the Galactic Council," said Varcus. "They'll decide if there's any reason not to evict you and your people."

"How long will I have to prepare? I mean, if we're leaving tomorrow morning, that doesn't give me much time to look for precedents, sleep, that sort of thing," I said.

"You can use the computer on my ship on the way if you like. But the hearing will be tomorrow afternoon, unless we aren't able to get enough council members off the puttering lawns," said Varcus.

"Any chance for a postponement?" I said.

"No," said Varcus.

"That's what I thought," I said. "Then can I at least bring someone with me? I could use some help on this, and Steve and I used to be a pretty good team. He'd do all the work and I'd take all the credit."

"You can bring anyone you like, Jake, within reason," said Varcus.

"Good. I'll bring Steve, then, if I can manage to get him on the ship. He's got a thing about flying, so space flight might be a toughie," I said.

Just then we heard the sound of a man and woman laughing and turned to look, and found Larry with two of his arms strategically placed around Paula as they stumbled towards his ship. The couple spied us and Paula smiled a mischievous smile and waved, as Larry gave us a two handed thumbs up. The door to his ship opened and they disappeared inside.

"And on that note," I said, turning and heading down the ramp and towards the farm house.

Varcus stood thinking about the broadcast he was going to have to give to the humans to explain the delay in their move, until Robb's mumbled hummings at his feet interrupted his train of thought. "And you! Robot!" he said. "Get inside before the neighbors see you!"

Chapter Sixteen

Cynthia sat on the sofa next to Nicole in the living room, surrounded by a healthy pile of wedding gifts. Steve sat on the floor nearby, already opened presents around him.

Cynthia ripped the wrapping off another box and examined at it. "Gee, a toaster; that'll be a big help on Gork," she said curtly, and tossed it to Steve who added it to his pile. She quickly picked up another present. "Let's see what we have next," she said, tearing into the paper. "Oh look. A ceramic rooster. That'll be a big help on Gork," she said, throwing it at Steve.

"Glad to see you're taking things so well," I said, from a safe distance across the room.

Cynthia looked at me. "My parents and most of my friends went home to pack for the move, so my gift opening party's a bust, there's a hung-over robot sleeping it off in the hammock in my backyard, and a few days from now I'll probably be running away from god knows what kind of alien creature instead of going down water slides in my bikini getting a tan. So yeah, overall I think I'm taking it pretty well."

"Are you sure you don't want to come to Kador with us? I feel bad stealing Steve away the day after your wedding," I said.

"No, I'll be fine here. Nicole and I can use a little girls with no aliens time. But if you run into Paula tell her I said to get her fanny home," said Cynthia.

"I wonder where they went," I said.

"Don't know," said Steve. "I went out early this morning to make sure the guys showed up to milk the cows, and Larry's ship was gone."

"I thought you were watching her, Nicole," I said. "If you knew she was going to get down with an alien anyway, the least you could have done was taken her and tossed her into Varcus' ship instead where she might have done us some good."

"It wasn't my fault. I turned my back for one second and they disappeared on me," said Nicole.

"I just hope they're here when we get back from this court thing. I don't have a clue what my argument is going to be and it'd be nice to have Larry's deal as a back-up plan if I can't fix this," I said. "Speaking of which, I suppose we better get going."

Nicole stood up and walked over to me while Steve kissed Cynthia goodbye. "I know you're nervous about the case, Jake."

"Actually I'm not, for some reason," I said.

"That's the spirit," said Nicole.

"No, I think that's the denial," I said. "Or Varcus' ray. Take your pick."

"You'll do fine. Here; take this with you. For luck," said Nicole.

"Ah, your digital camera. How sweet," I said.

"My *lucky* digital camera," said Nicole.

"And there's no hidden agenda here, is there? You don't want me to take this along so I'll bring you back a bunch of pictures of Kador or anything, do you?" I said.

"Nope. Just for luck," said Nicole.

"Right," I said. "Just be sure to mention me in your Pulitzer speech."

Nicole suddenly leaned over and gave me a peck on the cheek, not the worst thing to have had happen to me recently.

"Was that for luck too?" I said.

"No, the camera covered that," said Nicole.

"Then what was it for?" I asked.

"You figure it out," said Nicole, taking me by the shoulders, then turning me around and pushing me towards the door while I tried to do what she suggested.

"I hope I don't get space sick and barf all over Varcus' ship," said Steve, picking up his suitcase and following.

"The guy's throwing us off the Earth; as Representative, I happily grant you permission to decorate his interior with bacon and eggs," I said. "In fact, I encourage it."

I opened the door and walked out onto the porch, and found Johnny skateboarding up and down the sidewalk. "Dudes!" he said excitedly. "Varcus is gonna give us a tour of the solar system!"

Chapter Seventeen

"That's Mercury," I said, while gazing at the dusty looking brown and gold sphere rotating in front of us. I snapped yet another picture. "That's really the planet Mercury."

"You said the same thing when we came to Saturn, Jupiter, Venus, Mars..." said Steve.

"Yeah, I know. But it's Mercury," I said, still in awe of what I'd seen today. The planets had all been incredible, although Pluto had been a bit dull, which was why Varcus had zipped us out to it first so we could work our way back in towards the good stuff.

Saturn was simply glorious, and Jupiter had been absolutely spectacular. But it was our own little planet Earth that I'd found to be the most beautiful, a vibrant blue, green, and brown sphere of life, covered in swirling white clouds. Gazing at it I couldn't help feeling that if everyone on it had a chance to go into space and see it from that same perspective, they might just park their cars, at least for a while, and walk into the nearest rainforest and give a tree frog a hug. Of course they'd probably all keel over dead from the frog's poison a moment later, but the thought would have still counted.

"Hey, why don't you come over here? There's a much better view," I said to Steve, who was sitting in one of the chairs Varcus had formed along the center wall.

Varcus had taken the top down so everyone could get a better view, and it had been disconcerting at first flying through space without outer walls. But I'd gotten used to it, and was now standing next to where the domed hull should have been visible.

"No thanks," said Steve, one hand tightly gripping the arm of his chair, the other tightly gripping his silver foil barf bag. "I can see everything quite well from here."

"Coward," I said.

"Dudes, I'm flying the ship!" said Johnny's voice, coming over the loudspeaker system.

"On second thought, maybe I'll join you," I said. Varcus had invited Johnny up into the cockpit after being blackmailed by Robb into bringing him along on the trip, something about hiding the keys to the ship.

"Hey, will this thing go upside down?" we heard Johnny say.

"Let's not find out, shall we?" Varcus replied. *"Just follow the gauge and steer us out of the solar system."*

The door to the other half of the ship opened, and Robb came into the room and walked over to me. "I'm supposed to ask if you would like some refreshments," he whispered.

"I don't know, what do you have?" I said.

"Shush! Stop shouting!" said Robb.

"I'm not shouting," I said, as quietly as I could. "Still feeling a bit under the weather, are we?"

"More like I *am* the weather; something like a hurricane wrestling a tornado," said Robb. "I have calculated that my head feels like it is four point six times larger than it actually is."

"Why don't you just turn off your simulation circuits?" said Steve.

"Johnny told me not to. He said if I'm going to be a righteous dude I have to learn to own the pain," said Robb.

"I don't know; I'd consider myself the most righteous dude on Earth if I could shut off my hangover the next day," I said. "By the way, where did your clothes go?"

"Varcus made me put them in the washer," said Robb sulkily. "Although I have to admit they were smelling a bit gamey after last night."

The door opened and Varcus walked into the room. "You're not honestly leaving Johnny alone to steer the ship, are you?" I said.

"Yeah, he's not exactly Mister Sulu, you know," complained Steve, who was getting paler by the moment.

"You wouldn't say that if you had seen him play Asteroids at the Seven-Eleven," said Robb.

"He'll be fine," said Varcus. "He can't really do any harm, space being such a big place. Unless he decides to do a u-turn and plunge us into the sun, of course."

"I get the feeling he's liable to do that just for a thrill," I said.

"How did you two enjoy the tour?" asked Varcus.

"Seeing the planets was nice but I could have done without some of the maneuvers, like when we whipped that u-turn around Titan," said Steve.

"That was Johnny's idea," said Varcus. "He wanted to see if we'd start going back in time; something about beating someone named Tony Hawk to the punch and scoring with hordes of skater groupie chicks."

"The whole trip was absolutely amazing," I said. "Thank you, Varcus. You know it almost makes it worth being thrown off the Earth to see what we got to see today."

"You're most welcome," said Varcus. "I just came in to let you know I'll be displacing us into Kador's system momentarily and I should have us down on the ground in just a few moments."

"Thank God," said Steve, who planned to, the minute we landed.

"If we are landing in a few minutes then why did you send me in here to see if they wanted something to eat? I'm going to go check on my clothes," said Robb, and he turned and trudged back out of the room.

"Did you just say we're landing in a few minutes? I haven't had a chance to prepare for my case yet," I complained. "I've been too busy being the first human to see, well, stuff."

"I'm sorry, but with this displacement drive interstellar travel times are almost nil," said Varcus.

"Will I have any time after we land?" I said.

"Yes, you should have an hour or so before the hearing starts," said Varcus.

"Perfect. One hour to come up with a defense to save the planet," I said.

"You mean the people, don't you?" said Steve.

"I wish everyone would stop saying things like that!" I said.

"Hey, Varcus dude," said Johnny over the PA. *"There's like this really, really big blip on the radar in front of us coming up really, really fast; I think it might be a deathstar. What should I do?"*

"Oops. Maybe I better get up there," said Varcus, heading towards the door.

"Yeah, maybe you should do that," I said.

"Please let me stand on some ground just one more time, please let me stand on some ground just one more time..." repeated Steve over and over into his barf bag.

Chapter Eighteen

I pushed through the turnstile and into the main area of Kador Prime Spaceport, then stopped and looked around, wondering when and if I was ever going to wake up and get back to reality. "This is crazy," I said. "I'm standing here on an alien planet a zillion miles away from Earth, surrounded by hundreds of jet setting aliens and their luggage. Would somebody please explain to me how this happened?"

"You went off to pee," said Steve.

"Oh yeah. Remind me never to do that again," I said, as a Fandorian family of fifty-five flippered by.

"There he is," I heard someone say, and a weasely looking, furry brown alien dressed in a silver trench coat and hat pushed his way through the crowd, followed by a multi-limbed creature holding what looked like a camera, which he pointed at me.

"Who the hell are you?" I asked, suddenly feeling very irritable.

"Universe renowned reporter Bink Cruf here, bringing you another Mega News exclusive," said the weasel. "I'm here with Earth Representative Jake Williams, who has just arrived on Kador for his all important hearing before the Galactic Council. What do ya think, Jake, do you humans even stand a chance, or are you just trying to waste everyone's time?" he asked, shoving a microphone in my face.

I looked at him and said nothing. I'd had a few small dealings with the media before, and the nicest thing I could say was that I didn't want to be Facebook friends with most of them. But this Bink guy, I just hated him instantly for some reason. Intensely hated, as a matter of fact, more than any other person or creature I'd ever met, which seemed a little odd.

"No comment?" said Bink. "Then perhaps you'd like to say something about GREEN's damning report stating that humans are no good, self serving, cannibalistic, parasitical, toxic beings that go out of their way to kill and torture anything green and living."

"What? That's not what was in the report, was it?" I snapped, suddenly feeling an overwhelming urge to sound off. "Anyway, humans are nothing like that; well, most of them, at least."

"Are you saying your people *don't* terrorize and murder innocent dandelions?" asked Bink. "Go ahead, try to deny it."

"I'm not *going* to deny it, because dandelions are far from innocent and have it coming; they started the war by para-trooping into our yards and trying to establish a foothold," I growled, getting madder by the second and wishing there was a dandelion around to stomp on. "And get that microphone out of my face before I make you eat it!"

"Then how would you respond to the story that's about to break that you yourself have sexually abused forty-seven percent of Earth's ring tailed lemur population, and one blue whale who is now undergoing extensive psychotherapy?" said Bink, ignoring my threat.

"What freaking idiot's going to report that?" I shouted, feeling fully angry for the first time in days and quite enjoying the sensation.

"Yours truly, Bink Cruf, bringing you another Mega News exclusive," said Bink proudly.

"And who told you?" I almost roared, moving on from angry to enraged.

"I have my sources, and they've asked to remain anonymous," said Bink. "But back to the Earth; would you be willing to confirm that-"

I steamed for a moment, feeling like I was going to explode, then grabbed Bink around his rather skinny neck and pinned him against a nearby wall before he could finish. "How about you confirming who your source was for all this crap before *I* confirm that ringing your neck will shut you up," I said menacingly. I really felt like I wanted to kill him; I couldn't remember ever being so angry at anyone, but yet having it feel so good.

"Jake, please calm down; don't kill the nice, sleazy reporter," said Varcus.

145

"I'm guessing you don't have any kind of calming ray on me right now, Varcus, because I definitely and finally have some aggressive feelings going on!" I said, almost giddily.

"No, I can't use anything to pacify you, because it would affect everyone else here on Kador, too. The intense anger you're feeling at the moment is a whiplash effect from having your more violent emotions cooped up for the past few days. Normally I'd have weaned you off the ray, but I didn't have time," explained Varcus. "You should start feeling better shortly. Meanwhile, I'd consider it a personal favor to me if you would try and control your urges and not assault everyone you meet."

"Sorry, can't help you there. Not till I'm done with this guy, at least," I said.

"Well, I gave it my best shot," sighed Varcus. "I would suggest you tell him what he wants to know, Mr. Cruf. His species has a violence factor of nine point three on the Von Calix scale, and that's *without* the hunger for aggression he's built up over the past few days."

Bink gulped, which probably wasn't easy given the grip I had on his throat. "Alright," he squeaked. "It was my uncle Gurt who told me about the lemurs and the whale."

"And where did he hear it?" I demanded.

"How should I know? I don't ask my sources where they get their information; I just pay them for it," said Bink.

"Jake, you should know before you decide whether or not to strangle him that Bink's not the only vile and despicable reporter out there. Since everyone did away with their lawyers the media has gotten totally out of control," said Varcus. "They print or say whatever they want because there's no one left to sue them for liable."

"It's not that different on Earth even with lawyers; go ask Angelina and Brad," I said. With some mental effort I reluctantly let go of Bink and pushed him back into the crowd. "Wouldn't do any good to throttle you anyway; another three of you would just pop up in your place. Just get out of here before I go totally Sean Penn on you."

"You'll be sorry you did that, mister high and mighty Representative," said Bink. He turned to his camera squid. "Did you get all that?" he asked, as they retreated out of sight.

I stood fuming, but already feeling a bit calmer, maybe because I'd gotten some good old anger out of my system.

Steve walked up and put a comforting hand on my shoulder, and said, "I'm sure no one believes what those guys report anyway, Jake."

"Oh, people still believe it," said Varcus. "They believe it because-"

"Because it's on TV," I finished.

"Yes," said Varcus.

"Hail, citizens!" said Larry, suddenly arriving on the scene. He looked around him; "Hey, where did Bink go? I go to all the trouble of setting up an in-depth and heart wrenching interview and he cuts it short?"

"So it was *you* who did that?" I snapped, but it felt like a normal level of snappiness this time.

"Yes; no need to thank me too awfully much," said Larry.

"Thank you? Why the hell would I want to thank you for siccing a reporter on me, you lunatic!" I said.

"Because any publicity is good publicity," said Larry.

"Yeah, I'm sure the court will be more lenient on me if they think I'm a lemur molester," I said.

"Eww," said Larry. "I'm no PR Expert, but you should have reconsidered before going public with your closet full of skeletal mammal abuses."

"I didn't go public with it!" I said.

"Then where did you hear it?" said Larry.

"On TV, where else?" I said sarcastically.

"Then it must be true," said Larry.

"We'll circle back to that one later," I said. "In the mean time, what have you done with Paula?"

"It would be ungentlemanly of me to recount in depth my latest conquest to you at this time, but perhaps we can talk about it over drinks later," said Larry.

"I just want to know where she is; I have no desire to hear what you two have been doing," I said.

"Oh," said Larry, obviously crestfallen at my lack of interest in his juicy details. "She's over at the shoe mall right now. She seemed very content to graze there with my Federation Fortune credit stick for an hour or eight."

"You gave a woman your credit card and told her to go shop? You're even stupider than I thought," I said.

"Are you saying that was a defective idea?" asked Larry.

"I don't know about space women, but an Earth woman holding your bank account in her hand while walking around alien shoe stores filled with new types of shoes she's never seen before, kind of spells financial wrath on a biblical scale," I said.

"Hm. Then perhaps I should be more vigilant and keep her company while she shops; I do not wish to have my nest egg shattered into a bazillion pieces like that Humpty fellow from your planet's childhood legends," said Larry, and he scurried off back into the crowd.

Varcus looked at his watch. "Uh-oh; we're really running late now. That holding pattern we were stuck in ate up some of our time to begin with, and the line at decontamination didn't help either."

"That was a real treat, by the way; the guy could have at least warned me before he sprayed that crap all over me," I said.

"But it was necessary. You wouldn't want to wipe all us aliens out with some stray Earth disease, now would you?" asked Varcus.

"Is that a trick question?" I asked. "So what are you telling me? I'm not going to have any time to prepare for court at all now?"

"I'm saying we have twenty minutes to get you there or they're going to declare a forfeit," said Varcus.

"And I'm guessing they won't be the ones giving up," I said. "Then come on, let's go grab a taxi. I'm dying to see what kind of illegal aliens you have driving your cabs."

Chapter Nineteen

Steve, Varcus, and I stood in the corridor leading into the main forum of the Galactic Council, Robb having escorted Johnny to the hotel where we'd be staying that evening to avoid either of them causing any problems.

"You'll have to wait in one of the antechambers, Steve," said Varcus, indicating one of the doors lining the hallway.

"You mean he can't even come in with me?" I said. "I thought he was coming along to help. All he's been able to do so far is divide his breakfast up into little silver bags."

"Can I help it I forgot my Dramamine?" said Steve.

"Like that would have helped," I said. "You get motion sick on golf carts."

"I'm sorry, Jake. Only the Representative is allowed inside," said Varcus.

"I don't know if you've noticed, but you say *"I'm sorry"* an awful lot," I said. "Either you're overly sensitive, or you should rethink your lifestyle and try not to do so many things you need to apologize for in the first place."

"I don't think I'd be much help in there anyway," said Steve. "I've been racking my brain for some strategy for you to use but I've come up with a big fat lot of nothing."

"Same here, but if you'd been able to come along, the pictographs humans are going to scribble on the Gorkian cave walls before we all go extinct would have read *"Jake and Steve blew it."* Now they're only going to mention me," I said.

"Sorry," said Steve.

"Don't you start too," I said.

"Anyway, good luck, buddy," said Steve. "Give 'em hell."

"I'd love to, but I think we're going to end up being sent to it instead," I said.

Steve went into one of the waiting rooms, and Varcus and I continued down the stone hall towards a large ornate archway. We walked through it and came out onto the main floor of the forum of the Galactic Council. It reminded me of a Greek senate; a large round room with seats going upwards like a small basketball stadium, the ceiling an arched glass dome through which poured golden Kadorian sunlight.

"So this is a jury of my peers," I said, looking around the coliseum at the sea of two hundred or so wise looking, white skinned, white haired, white robed, androgynous beings that filled it.

"Pardon me?" said Varcus.

"An Earth expression. Being judged by a jury of your peers. And I'm not really sure this qualifies," I explained and complained.

"These are still your peers," said Varcus. "We're all connected throughout the universe as sentient beings."

"If you say so. But I'm a little surprised; I thought this was a *Galactic* Council. They all look like they're from the same species to me," I said.

"Ah. I suppose that is confusing to you," said Varcus. "Let me explain. The beings you see are not really here."

"So it's like our government back in the US; when they bother to show up they spend most of their time having affairs with pages or roaming the halls looking for special interest groups who'd like to donate to their reelection fund," I said.

"No, I mean they're not physically here," said Varcus. "These are all holographic representations. You could call them avatars."

"Only if you feel like tangling with James Cameron's legal team," I said.

"Then call them representatives of representatives," said Varcus. "You see that person over there, for instance?"

"You mean the one who looks identical to the person sitting next to him, who looks identical to the one next to him, and the one next to him, and the one next to him, etc, etc, etc?" I asked. "Or are they all hers? I can't even tell."

"Yes, that's the one," said Varcus. "He or she could be anywhere right now. In his office on Plankin, at her summer cottage on Drevd, or at his mistresses' hideaway on Baylon. And they could be anybody."

"I'm confused," I said. "Why would they be someone besides who they are?"

"When a session such as this is called, a representative goes into a closed room wherever they're physically located," said Varcus. "The room will always have a chair, a holographic camera, and a view screen so he, she, or he-she can see the goings on here. The camera captures the person's words and movements and relays them, and they are displayed as one of the figures you now see in the council room."

"Is that so they don't have to actually be here?" I asked.

"Partially. Even though interstellar travel is now quite fast it's still fairly expensive," said Varcus. "But mostly it's done this way to provide anonymity for the council members."

"Anonymity? You mean you don't even know how your representatives vote?" I said.

"For the most part, no," said Varcus. "A computer filters out any names, phrases, or gestures they might let slip that would give away who they are."

"But that's ridiculous," I said. "They could be voting against everything they said they supported when they ran for office. Providing they even run for office out here, that is."

"And how is that any different from your own government?" said Varcus.

"Alright; you got me there. But at least on Earth we know they lied," I said. "I don't see how this is any kind of improvement."

"Here on the council everyone is able to vote for something because they think it's right, and not because they feel obligated to due to their party affiliation, or because of someone who helped put them into office. Oh, everyone has something they stand for and tend to support, but when a good idea comes along that belongs to someone else they don't vote against it simply because the other guys want it," said Varcus. "They don't even know which guys are the other guys."

"Interesting," I said. "I guess I can see the advantages. But it must be frustrating for your poor special interest groups. On Earth if you give a guy a couple of million dollars you expect him to allow you to continue to dump chemicals into the Mississippi River. Here he might shut you down and you'd never even know he was the one who did it."

"Yes," said Varcus. "Too bad, eh?" A bell sounded three times and Varcus straightened his suit. "This is it, Jake. Are you ready?"

"No," I said, never being more sure of anything in my life.

"Good," said Varcus. "I'll be right beside you. I can't argue for you or act as a witness, but as Earth's sponsor I can answer informational questions regarding the case, and any procedural inquiries you might have."

I took a deep, nervous breath. Maybe it was because I was no longer under the influence of the pacifier ray, and there wasn't the frantic pace of a wedding to distract me. Or perhaps it was because I felt like I was about to go into court, which instinctively told me it was time to get serious. Whatever the reason, in that one breath, I finally felt some of the weight of what was happening, and what was at stake, bearing down on me, and I wished it was someone else who was standing there on Kador. But whether I liked it or not, I was the Representative, and there was no way to forestall the inevitable. "Okay; let's get this over with," I said.

Varcus led me into the center of the forum, and onto a slightly raised circular platform of red stone. "Members of the council, this is Jake Williams, Representative of the planet Earth," he said, his voice somehow amplified. "He has come before you today as is his right, to plead his case in the pending eviction proceedings against the humans of his world. Jake?"

I thought for a moment, then said to the council members, "Am I allowed to ask you a question?"

"A question?" asked one of them. "That would depend. Why don't you simply ask and we will see."

"Alright," I said. "Here goes; why are you moving us?"

"Why? I thought that was fairly obvious," said a council member.

"Not really. Being from Earth I don't know anything about your laws, or even if this has to do with a law. All I know is there was the report from GREEN, a decision of some kind was made to move us, and I was lucky enough to be the one served with the notice. But that doesn't tell me anything about whether or not it's legal," I said.

"I assure you, it is," said a council member.

"No offense, but your assurances don't do much to assure me," I said. "I'd like to know exactly what gives you the legal right to do this."

"Very well," said a council member. "We have a statute in our laws, code one thousand, seven hundred and sixty-four, that not only gives us the right, but compels us to do whatever we deem necessary to protect a life supporting planet, especially from its own inhabitants."

"Even if it puts those inhabitants in danger?" I said. "From what I've heard, this Gork you're trying to move us to isn't very hospitable."

"No, it is in fact quite a harsh place," admitted a council member.

"That's what I was afraid of," I said. "So you put the well being of a sphere of rock ahead of that of living, breathing, thinking beings?"

"A life sustaining planet such as the Earth also lives and breathes," said a council member. "And it supports countless numbers of creatures besides those that have become "civilized" who rely on it to sustain them. Unfortunately it can't defend itself."

"But it can't think and feel like a human can," I said. "Sentient beings-"

"-are overrated," said a council member. "There have been a great many whom the galaxy would have been far better off without."

"But we're people, and we deserve to be treated better than this," I said. "What you're about to do to us is simply not right."

"Mr. Williams, the ethics of our law are not in question here. We are not sacrificing your people; you will have a new home and your race will survive if they work hard enough. We do value life," said a council member. "And if that is all you came here to say we'll be adjourning quite quickly."

I decided to try a new angle. "Well, how about this, then; we humans had no say in this statute of yours. Where I come from we all vote together on issues, then live by the results."

"Really?" said a council member. "So I gather the American Indians, the Aborigines, and other races on the Earth all sat down with you and voted to be pushed aside and/or massacred to make way for what was considered to be the needs of the others? And what about the countless species of animals that no longer exist because of your people; did they get a vote as well? We do know something of your planet's history and its people, you know; we wouldn't make such a decision without study first."

"You know about all that, do you?" I said, disappointed. "But look, every species fights for its own survival, doesn't it?" I said. "And often at the expense of another. There were a lot of animals that disappeared long before we humans arrived on the scene."

"Perhaps, but that's not really why we're choosing to move you now, anyway; it's just an indication of your human level of concern for other beings," said a council member. "The problem is, you're affecting the planet itself on a grand scale, and it's threatening to alter it forever. And you know this, yet you continue to ignore the problem because it would be too inconvenient not to. You'd happily wipe out all life on Earth, including even your own species, to do what you think is best for you."

"But that should be our right," I said.

"You humans do go on and on about your rights, don't you?" said a council member. "Unfortunately, what you might consider to be your right is not always right."

"But you're throwing us off our planet!" I said passionately, a bit exasperated at not having any idea of what else to say. "We're thinking, feeling, sentient beings!"

"Yes, and if humans found that hedgehogs could think and feel just like you do, but were an imminent threat to your world, you would show no hesitation in either moving them or wiping them out, would you? That's all that we are doing," said a council member.

"But we've begun to make environmental progress now," I argued. "I admit it's come fairly slowly, and maybe later than it should have, but at least it's started; we just need more time."

"I'm sorry, but GREEN's report clearly states that having taken into account the calculations regarding the state of the environment, your so called progress, and the social, economic, and governmental factors guiding your race, that it is impossible for your people not only to fix things but to avoid doing irreparable damage to the planet in the near future," said a council member. "There is nothing you can say to convince us otherwise."

I sighed. I could tell I was going to get nowhere; the council's minds were made up. "That's what this really all about isn't it?" I said. "That damned report. A bunch of numbers, graphs and pie charts."

"There are no pie charts in the report, Jake" interjected Varcus helpfully.

"Thanks for clearing that up, Varcus" I said. "You know what? You got me; you got all of us, in fact. We're human. We make mistakes, and sometimes they're whoppers. We tried to make life on Earth better for the majority of us, and maybe we did go about it all wrong. So go ahead and do what you're going to do, because I'm obviously not going to be able to change your minds."

"Are you saying you're withdrawing your plea, Mr. Williams?" asked a council member.

"In a minute," I said. "First I want to tell you how impressed I was on the ride over here from the spaceport on the monorail. Your city is so beautiful, so clean. The air here is incredible. And Varcus tells me that you recycle ninety-seven percent of your waste?"

"That is correct," said a council member proudly.

"That's wonderful," I said. "Yours is definitely an ancient and wise culture."

"Thank you, Mr. Williams," said a council member.

"But I do have to ask you one last question if I may," I said.

"As you wish," said a council member.

"How long has GREEN been investigating planets?" I said.

"A little over two hundred years," said a council member. "Why?"

"Two hundred years, huh?" I said. "Not really that long in the scheme of things is it? I wonder how long it took to get Kador in the environmentally sound condition it's in today."

"What are you getting at?" asked a council member.

"I'm just wondering what this planet and the planets *you* all come from were like when all of *your* species were at where we humans are in *our* technological age. It's probably a good thing for you that GREEN wasn't up and doing their investigations back then, isn't it?"

"Why do you say that?" said a council member.

"Otherwise Gork would be a pretty crowded place by now, wouldn't it? Because I'm guessing you didn't all slither out of the muck, stand upright, and start recycling programs. Luckily, there was no around back then to decide whether or not *your* species were going to get their act together and stop polluting your worlds, so you had time to figure things out on your own. I guess what I'm saying is it's very advanced of you to expect more from others than from yourselves. And easy. But you all be sure and have a great and happy Kador day," I said, before turning and walking angrily out of the council room.

I stomped into the antechamber where Steve sat waiting, slammed the door behind me with a bang, and stood there, fuming.

Steve watched me calmly for a moment or two, then said cheerfully "So how did it go?"

"Were you ever sent to the principal's office when you were a kid?" I asked.

"No," said Steve. "I didn't get into any trouble until I met you."

"Remind me to make you thank me for that someday," I said. "But that's what it was like; you walk into the room and it doesn't matter what you say. She's the teacher, you're just a student, and you shouldn't have crazy glued everything to her desk. The principal's mind is already made up, and you're getting punished."

"So what you're trying to tell me is we're still getting punished?" said Steve.

"Yeah, looks like we'll all be serving detention time together on Gork," I said.

The door opened and Varcus came into the room.

"Don't even think about saying you're sorry," I said.

"I wasn't planning to," said Varcus. "You did what you could, Jake. That was what I was trying to tell you last night, about the hearing being pointless. Your eviction is based on the findings of the report, and unless you could refute them somehow no one was going to change their minds. I'm sorry."

"Just couldn't help yourself, could you?" I said. "It's not your fault, though. Screwing up the environment was our doing, and ruthlessly throwing us out of it is that self righteous council's."

"If it's any consolation, they were impressed by your closing argument," said Varcus.

"But it didn't change their minds, did it?" I said.

"No. Actually, they told me it strengthened their case," said Varcus. "There are a number of planets that have been discovered that are now void of life, or void of the life they once had, anyway, due to environmental changes brought on by their former inhabitants. The council said they only wished GREEN had been around at the time to save those planets as well. But they were still impressed that you at least seemed to understand that environmental problems could be caused by any race, even if you didn't think anyone should do anything about it."

"I never said that no one should do anything, I just said...oh, never mind. What's the difference? We're pretty much screwed now, aren't we?" I said. "I just can't believe I gave up so quickly in there."

"I'm sure you did everything you could," said Steve.

"Did I?" I said. "I remember divorce cases where I'd argue for hours to get a stupid plant or something for my client. And this was for the Earth; all of it! But I think maybe that was part of the problem. It was just too damned big."

"Don't beat yourself up, Jake," said Varcus. "There was nothing you could have done. Just try and keep that in mind. Being the Representative really only means that you're the one human we communicate and deal with, and not that you have the power to change anything. Everything has already been decided." He shrugged, and looked sympathetic. "I'll take you to your hotel so you can rest, and in the morning we'll go back to Earth."

"For now," I said. "Just don't unpack your bags; we won't be staying long."

Maybe I hadn't had the power to change anything like Varcus had said. But then again, I was the *only* person who was in the position to change that very thing, to find a way *to* have the power. I didn't think I'd ever get another chance to try, but I vowed if I ever did, things were going to be different next time.

Chapter Twenty

I switched off the Multi-Sensory Uberdef Super Surround 4D Picture Plasmoid TV after watching my interview with Bink for the third time. "That's about enough of that," I said. "It's amazing how quickly you can get sick of yourself, especially from every conceivable angle."

"Try telling that to Charlie Sheen," said Steve, taking a sip out of a bottle of something blue from the Translation Hotel mini-bar. He stood up; "I'm gonna go see if I can find an ice machine around here. This Workleberry juice isn't half bad, but it's awfully warm. Do you need anything, Jake?"

"Do you really have time to wait while I answer that question in its entirety?" I said.

"Never mind," said Steve. "Johnny, how about you? Johnny? Yo, Johnny..." he said to Johnny, who was sitting over in a corner playing with a hand held device of some sort.

"No, I'm good," said Johnny finally.

"I'll be right back," said Steve. He walked over to the door and pressed the open button but the door didn't seem to care. He pushed it again, and again, then again but the door continued to ignore him. "Okay, I guess I won't be right back. I seem to be having problems with leaving so maybe I shouldn't push myself that hard."

"What's wrong?" I asked.

"I think the door's broken," said Steve.

I got up and walked over to investigate. I pushed the open button, then did it again, and again, and again, as if repeating the same action over and over that already hadn't worked for Steve was going to help. "I think you're right, although I thought doors were one of the few things that couldn't *be* broken."

"Progress, I guess," said Steve.

"Is the light green or red?" asked Johnny, without looking up from whatever it was he was doing.

Steve examined the panel on the wall. "Red," he said.

"That means it's locked, dudes" said Johnny.

"So how do you unlock it?" I asked.

"If it's locked from the inside you push the open button," said Johnny.

"We have been, but it's not listening. How do we get its attention?" said Steve.

"Then it's probably locked from the outside again," said Johnny.

"What?!" said Steve. "You mean we're locked in here?"

"Affirmative," said Johnny calmly.

"How the hell did that happen?" I said.

"Varcus did it to keep us from wandering around," said Johnny.

"Why that little purple..." I said. "Now I'm angry. I could've maybe lived with them throwing us off the Earth, but now they're locking us in kitschy hotel rooms."

"Yeah, I feel kind of insulted. I don't know about you, but I wasn't even planning on wandering around," said Steve. "I didn't want to get in any trouble."

"What a shock," I said. "I wasn't planning on it either, though, but now that I'm locked in I want to wander all over the place. Maybe we could break a window."

"And then what? Shimmy down the side of the building one hundred and eighty-seven stories? No thank you. I get dizzy just looking out the window," said Steve.

"And another shock," I said.

"Dudes; chill," said Johnny.

"I don't feel like chilling," I said. "I'm sure you'd be content to just sit there and play video games all day, but I want out of here now that I can't *get* out of here."

"I'm not playing video games," said Johnny.

"Then what's that you're messing with?" said Steve. "You know, you could try doing something useful for a change."

Just then the door they had been arguing with slid open, and Robb stepped into the room. "Well, are you coming out or not?" he said.

"Dude," said Johnny to Steve. "You were saying?"

"So you can talk to Robb on that thing, Johnny?" I asked, as we exited the hotel lobby doors and entered onto Alpha Rudolpho Boulevard.

"Si; Robb gave it to me in case I needed anything," said Johnny. "It was an accessory that came with him when he was purchased so his owner could communicate with him, but Varcus just uses his PED instead."

"You two are getting to be good friends, aren't you?" said Steve.

"He's my bro," said Robb, dressed again in his new old clothes.

"Robb's pretty cool for a machine," said Johnny.

"Probably because he wasn't programmed by Bill Gates," I said. "Although I wondered there for a while."

"Johnny's teaching me to chill out," said Robb.

"That's what I need to do now, too," said Johnny.

"You? What's wrong with you?" asked Steve.

"They confiscated my skateboard at the spaceport," said Johnny, like totally bummed out. "That customs lizard dude said it was illegal contraband."

"Are they going to give it back to you when we leave the planet?" I asked.

"Yeah, but I don't have it with me now. We've never been apart for so long," said Johnny.

"Gee, that's too bad," said Steve, managing to come close to approaching being able to sound sincere. "So now what?"

"That's a good question," I said, wondering what to do now that we were standing on an alien street instead of being locked in an alien hotel room. "My plan only went as far as getting to the other side of our hotel room door; I've been winging it ever since."

I looked around at the capital city of Kador Prime. It wasn't really all that different from Chicago, other than the fact that it was very clean, had no cars driving on its streets, and had beings milling about from every corner of the galaxy instead of every corner of the world. The buildings were still tall and glassy, just shiny and spacier looking and about a hundred stories taller, so that they blotted out even more of the sky. I took out the camera and snapped a quick picture of the city for Nicole, then put it away again. "I don't know about anybody else, but I could use a beer."

"Why not? After all, we are on an alien planet with a thousand new wonders to see. Might as well go sit in a bar and get drunk instead," said Steve.

"That's what I was thinking. Besides, maybe they'll have a thousand new alcoholic wonders to drink," I said. "Robb, do you have any idea where there might be a good place around here? And please don't tell me this is a dry planet or I'm definitely going to lose it."

Robb shrugged. "How should I know? I just had my first drink yesterday."

"I know, but can't you interface with some central computerized Yellow Page directory or something?" I asked.

"Who do I look like, R2-D2?" said Robb.

"How do you know about him?" asked Steve.

"I inputted all of Johnny's DVDs into my memory banks," said Robb.

"I suppose I can just ask someone," I said. I looked over the crowd going by, trying to find someone who didn't look like they would just as soon excrete alien mucus over me as to talk to me. "Excuse me, err sir," I said, hoping to at least get that part right. "Can you tell me if there's a good bar around here?"

The being stopped and turned, and four eyes glared at me. "Sir?! Hmpf. Some nerve. Just ignore me why don't you?" said one of its two heads in a decidedly female voice.

"Yes, that's my wife you're not talking to," said the other head in a masculine tone. "If I had time I'd teach you some manners."

"I'm sorry. I didn't see your other head," I said.

The alien harrumphed and twirled around and stomped haughtily off.

"What the hell was that all about?" I asked.

"That was a Pairadian husband and wife," said Larry. "They share a body at marriage."

"I bet that's a messy divorce," I said. "Hey wait a minute, where did you come from?"

"The spaceport," said Larry.

"Still? What, did you get lost? I thought you were going to go shopping with Paula," I said.

"I did, but she became agitated when I asked a Nerokian sales girl for her number," said Larry sulkily. "And then after I told a Gradoll chick she had nice figures she made me take her home."

"You hit on two other women while you were with Paula?" said Steve.

"No, four," said Larry. "Would you like to hear about the other two, too?"

"Thanks, maybe later," said Steve.

"So is she at your place then?" I asked.

"I don't have a place here; they revoked my alien citizenship years ago," said Larry. "I took Paula home home, back to Earth. That's why I was coming from the spaceport." He sniffed. "I miss her already!"

"How did you know where to find us?' asked Steve.

"Where else would you be?' asked Larry.

"Never mind that," I said, now wanting a drink more than ever. "We still need to find a bar. I don't suppose you have suggestions, do you Larry?"

"Rokko's. Two blocks that way, one block left," said Larry. He checked one of his watches. "Happy hour starts in six minutes."

"Alright everyone, this way. Stay together and don't look the aliens in the eye, no matter how many they have," I said, heading down the street. "Your Representative's only head needs numbing."

Chapter Twenty One

My posse and I plunked down around a large, round table in Rokko's Lounge. I picked up a table tent and looked it over, unable to recognize anything on it. "So what's good here, Larry?' I asked.

"I don't know: I've never been to this place," said Larry.

I stared at him. "Then why did you suggest we come here?"

"Because when you asked me about a bar there was a sign across the street from where we were standing that said, "*Come to Rokko's Lounge, best happy hour in town starting at six o'clock. Ladies night every Tuesday,*" said Larry.

Robb suddenly made an odd beeping sound.

"Excuse you," I said. "You need a Tums or something?"

"No, I'm fine. Fartus is paging me though," said Robb. He sat with his head cocked to one side as if listening. "He's at the hotel. He wants to know where the photon everyone went. Should I tell him to go engage himself in some lewd bodily function?"

"Thanks, but you can go ahead and tell him where we are," I said. "We're not hiding, we're just not sitting back in that room just because he wants us too."

"Okay," said Robb, sending off a message back to Varcus.

"Hello, boys," said a tall, willowy, green waitress with long, flowing, golden hair, sparkling light blue eyes, and big round ears like a teddy bear. "My name is Cleeva, and I'll be your waitress. Would you like to hear our-" She stopped in mid-sentence when she looked at me, and her eyes grew wide in recognition. "You're the human from Earth! The one who-"

"I don't molest lemurs!" I protested.

"I can vouch for that," said Steve.

"Oh," said Cleeva. "And that other creature?"

"Wouldn't even know where to start with a whale," I said.

"That I can't verify; he could have looked it up on Wikipedia," said Steve.

Cleeva tsked and looked irritated. "Isn't that just like the news today?" she said, disapprovingly. "Always just making things up for ratings. So what can I get for you gentlemen?"

"Margaritas!" said Robb enthusiastically.

"What?" Cleeva asked.

"Tequila?" said Robb hopefully.

"I don't think we have that," said Cleeva.

"Bummer," said Robb depressingly, finishing his sprint through the emotions.

"Do you have anything that resembles beer?" I asked.

Cleeva thought for a moment. "I don't know what beer is but how about a couple of beakers of Fleb?"

I looked over at Larry who I thought, despite all previous indications to the contrary, was most likely to be of help here.

"Fleb. It's cold and fizzy and people drink it while watching sports," said Larry.

"Sounds like a winner. A couple of pitchers of Fleb then," I said.

"Beakers," said Larry.

"Whatever," I said.

"What kind of Fleb do you want?' asked Cleeva.

"You mean, do I want the king of Flebs, a light Fleb that tastes great and is less filling, or a Fleb that actually has some taste and wouldn't make an Irishman gag?" I asked.

"I mean do you want Alpha, Beta, or Gamma Fleb?" asked Cleeva.

"What's the difference?" asked Steve.

"If you're going to be operating power tools later, you'll want to stick with Alpha Fleb. If you're out for a good time, good conversation, and a warm fuzzy glow with semi-decent hand-eye coordination, then I would suggest Beta Fleb," explained Cleeva. "But if you just lost your girl, your job-"

"Your skateboard," said Johnny.

"Your planet," said Steve.

"-then you probably want to say the hell with my higher brain functions and ability to walk, just give me some Gamma Fleb," said Cleeva.

"That's a no brainer then, or hopefully will be," I said. "Gamma Fleb porfavor, senorita."

"Coming right up," said Cleeva, turning and heading towards the bar.

"Hey, how did she know what I meant?" I said. "I was speaking Spanish."

"But she probably heard Poota, her own language, unless she happens to speak something else," said Larry. "There are translator satellites orbiting this and every other planet in SOW."

"SOW?" asked Steve.

"Yes, one of those pig things you'll be representing in court in Annandale," I said.

"Would've been representing in court, you mean," said Steve.

"SOW stands for Society of Worlds," said Larry.

"Catchy," I said. "So it didn't matter what I spoke, English, Spanish, Pig-Latin or Swahili, it was going to come out as Poota to her?"

"Yes," said Larry. "Varcus and I use personal versions when we travel."

"We could have used one of those over the Earth so we could understand what the hell those foreign telemarketers were trying to sell us," I said.

"How are we going to pay for all this?" asked Steve, realizing the translator probably wasn't going to be able to do convert the greenbacks they were carrying.

"Crap! I suppose my platinum card isn't going to impress them much here is it?" I said.

"Maybe I can help," said Larry. "Jake, have you decided about my generous offer to gallantly save everyone on your planet yet?"

"No, and I really don't want to talk about it right now other than to say that it's looking a helluva lot better at this point," I said.

"I am glad to hear it. But we just did. Talk about it, that is. Now I can write the evening off on my taxes as a legitimate business expense, so everything's on me," said Larry.

"You still pay taxes out here? I thought you were all *so* advanced," said Steve

"No one's that advanced," said Larry.

I surveyed the room to gather important drinking information, such as where the bathrooms were in case Fleb used the same fast track route through the body as beer. I made a mental note that they were next to the table in the far corner and was about to rejoin my own table's conversation, when I noticed that the three spiked

179

aliens sitting there in business attire were all talking, but apparently not to one another. I wondered stupidly at first if it wasn't some form of telepathy, then decided it wasn't important anyway, until I glanced around and found that many of the other beings in the bar were doing the same thing. "Larry; why are so many people in here talking to themselves? Are they sharing a brain or something?"

"Some of them might be. But most of them are just talking on their self fones," said Larry.

"Self phone? Oh, you mean like cell phones," I said. "I suppose I can't see them because they're so small and hiding in their ears or something."

"No, you can't see them because they're so small and hiding in their brains," said Larry. "Many people choose to have self fones installed in their children at birth."

"That's terrible!" said Steve.

"Best way to stay connected," said Larry.

"Do you have one?" I asked.

"I used to, but I had it removed because my manly chin was blocking reception," said Larry. "Now I have to use my PED. Who knows what important details I might be missing about my friends lives, such as what they are having for dinner or what cute thing their kidling just did to the family catoid."

Cleeva came back with glasses and two big beakers of a red colored, bubbly liquid, and put them on the table. "If you want me to start you a tab I'll need someone's credit stick in case you all pass out," she said, and Larry handed his to her and she moved on to another table.

"Thank the spirits I got that away from Paula when I did," said Larry. "You were right, Jake. She was glad to see me because she was having trouble carrying everything, and she said with my four muscular arms she was finally going to be able to do some real power shopping."

"I told you so," I said.

Larry sniffled again. "But I still miss her," he said sadly. "She did this thing with her hair where she twirled it around her finger and this thing with her tongue where she twirled it around-"

"Agh! Stop right there. That's too much information," I said, grabbing a beaker, then filling up glasses and passing them around.

"-her spoon when she ate Bolarian Mint freeze," finished Larry, ignoring my request for conversation brakes. "That was too much information?"

"From you, yes," I said. "But then pretty much everything is."

"And if you like Paula so much then stop hitting on other women all the time!" snapped Steve irritably.

"What's gotten into you all of a sudden?" I said.

"I miss Cynthia," said Steve. "It's the day after my wedding and she's light years away, and this bonehead keeps complaining that the gorgeous woman he's infatuated with is mad at him because he can't stick to just her."

"It would be selfish of me to keep myself to myself," protested Larry. "And I'm not a bonehead."

"Yes you are," I said, holding up my glass and examining it. "Well, it looks more or less entirely unlike beer," I said, then took a tentative taste. "Hmm."

"Well?" said Steve, not about to touch the stuff until someone else tried it and refrained from spitting it across the table or having their head explode.

"And yes, it doesn't taste like beer, either," I said.

"It doesn't taste like tequila, either," said Robb sulkily, after sampling his.

I tried it again. "Actually it tastes a little like Coke."

"Coke Coke or coke coke?" said Steve suspiciously. "As in, am I supposed to drink it or sniff it?"

"Or lick it off the bar," said Robb.

I looked at Robb but decided I didn't want to know. "It just tastes kind of like a cola. Try it."

Steve picked up his glass and gave it a sip. "You're right, it does."

"I guess the big brewers out here in Futurama finally got beer to taste exactly like pop," I said.

"Actually Float Cola and Beeb Beer merged after the great beer and cola wars of the thirties," said Larry. "They were the giants left standing in their respective industries, and when they finally made peace they combined their products into one."

"So you used to have real beer out here in la la land?" I asked.

"Yes. Sadly it's gone. Earth is one of the last backwater places you can still find it,' said Larry.

"For the next two days or so," said Steve.

Just then Varcus stormed into the bar and up to the table. "There you are! I'm very angry with all of you. Especially you, robot, for letting them out."

"So what else is new?" said Robb in his recently learned who gives a flying whatever voice.

"Get up. You're all going straight back to the hotel," said Varcus.

"But I don't have a room there," said Larry.

"Not you, you idiot!" said Varcus. "Everyone but Larry. Come on. Now. Up. Let's go."

The table ignored him and sat drinking their Flebs.

"Stand up. Time to go. Gotta get a move on. Can't have you Earthlings all exposed to oh the hell with it," said Varcus, and he pulled a chair over from a nearby table and sat down with his not to be moved charges.

"Cleeva! Another glass over here," I said.

"I suppose it's happy hour isn't it?" asked Varcus. He looked around the table and found a lot of somber faces. "Maybe not. What's wrong?"

"Let's see," I said. "Larry misses Paula, Steve misses Cynthia, Johnny misses Rosebud, Fleb isn't tequila, and I screwed the pooch in court today so I'm going to go down in history as the person who lost the Earth once and for all. Does that about cover it?"

"I think I'm developing a rash, too," said Larry.

"Again with the too much information from you," I said. "But anyway, we're all going to get drunk. Good and drunk."

"Gamma Fleb?" asked Varcus, looking at my glass.

"You got it," I said.

"Well, I just got chewed out by the council for bringing you here, so I'm not having the best of days either," said Varcus.

"I thought it was our right to have a hearing," said Steve.

"It is, but you aren't supposed to know about it and just because someone's robot blabbed about it doesn't mean the council is very happy with me that you found out," said Varcus.

"Live with it, dude," said Robb.

"And his name is Robb," said Johnny.

Varcus sighed. "Fine; I'm tired of arguing about it. From now on I promise to call you Robb."

"Then we're cool," said Robb.

"Good," said Varcus.

"For now," said Robb.

Varcus shook his head. "You know, I remember when my life used to make some kind of sense," he said, as Cleeva dropped off another glass at the table.

"Welcome to the club," I said, pouring Varcus a Fleb and sliding it towards him.

"I really shouldn't," said Varcus.

"Drink," I said, taking a sip of my own.

"This is Gamma Fleb, and I have to fly tomorrow," said Varcus.

"Drink," said Steve.

"And what if someone with authority comes in here and sees me drinking with a bunch of Earthlings who aren't even supposed to be on the planet, let alone in one of its bars," said Varcus.

"Wuss," said Robb.

Varcus glared at him. "Fine. I'm just having one though," he said. "There is no way I'm getting totally wonkered tonight."

Chapter Twenty Two

"You're wrong! You're absholutely wrong!" slurred Varcus. "The shecond Alien movie was directed by James Cameron, not Ridley Shcott," he said.

"Are you shure?" said Larry, equally inebriated.

"Absholutely," said Varcus.

"How do you two aliens know so much about Earth movies?' I asked, quite happy in the head myself, but still able to speak relatively clearly after years of intensive martini training.

"HBO, Cinemax, Turner Clashics," said Varcus. "They're all eashy to pick up in space off the Earth communications shyshtem."

"Don't forget the Playboy channel," said Larry.

Varcus reached out and managed to grab the beaker from the center of the table on only his second attempt, and tried to pour himself his ninth Fleb of the evening, but only a couple of drops dribbled out. "Dang it! Out again."

"More Fleb!" shouted Larry, who was turning out to be exactly the kind of drunk I'd feared he would.

Steve started snoring again, and I lightly whacked him on the back of his head. "Wake up."

"But I'm tired!" complained Steve, opening his eyes and yawning.

"All this started the last time you passed out on me, so you can just push through tonight," I said. "What we need is some music to liven things up."

"There is music," said Johnny.

I listened. "You call that music? And this is about the fifth time I've heard that same song. You could try playing something different next time on the jukebox."

"Dude, I did," said Johnny, who had switched from Fleb to Neutron Energy drink, and was now as wired as he'd ever been in his entire life, which was saying something. "I didn't know what to play so I just picked six different songs by six different people."

"More Fleb!" shouted Larry, drawing a few more glares from various aliens around the bar.

"They all sounded the same to me," I said.

"They are the shame," said Varcus. "More or less. The mushic industry started playing it safer and shafer, putting out mushic that fit a proven formula. They're down to one song now that they jusht change a little bit each time shomeone puts it out."

"Always wondered and worried what the future of Earth music was going to be like," I said. "Now I know. Probably a good thing we're being put out of our misery before we get any further down that road ourselves."

Cleeva brought two more beakers of Fleb over and put them on the table.

187

"Thank you," I said.

"You're very welcome," said Cleeva, a bit of flirt in her voice.

"More Fleb!" shouted Larry.

"Dude! Look in front of you," said Johnny, who in spite of his uber laid back persona was also beginning to get irritated with Larry.

"I know; it's more Fleb!" said Larry happily. "That's what I said."

Steve watched Cleeva walk away, then turned and looked at me. "She's pretty isn't she? In a greenish sort of way."

"Who, Cleeva? I guess she is," I said.

"I didn't know about the ears at first, but they grow on you," said Steve. "They're kinda cute."

"I suppose so," I said.

"I think she likes you," said Steve.

"Maybe," I said.

"Are you going to go for it?" said Steve.

"Aren't you the one who's always telling me I'm going to get in trouble if I keep messing around with so many women?" I said. "And now you want to know if I'm going to pick up some alien chick in a bar?"

"Well? Are you?" asked Larry.

"No," I said. "I wasn't planning on it."

"Good. I didn't want to break your heart when I shtole her out from under your nasal orifice," said Larry, taking a drink of Fleb but missing his mouth and pouring most of it down his chin and blue silk shirt.

"Yeah, you're just oozing sex appeal right now," I said.

"Thanksh," said Larry, stuffing a whopping handful of some greasy sauce covered Spam like meat balls into his mouth.

"Oh, I get it," said Steve.

"Get what?" I asked.

"I get why you're not interested in a hot, green, alien chick with cute ears," said Steve.

"I suppose you're going to tell me, aren't you," I said.

"You've got a thing for Nicole, don't you?" said Steve.

"No I don't!" I protested.

"Sure you do. I've seen the way you two look at each other," said Steve.

"Why, how does she look at me?" I asked, interestingly.

"See? You love her don't you," said Steve.

"Now you're just being stupid," I said.

"Jake and Nicole, sitting in a tree, k-i-s-s-i-n-g," sang Steve.

"First of all, there aren't going to be any trees to sit in pretty soon," I said. "At least not friendly Earth type ones. And second, shut-up or I'm telling Cynthia about your Jessica Alba dreams when we get back." Steve immediately stopped sing-songing and I was left with the jukebox, which I found was almost worse. "Can't we do anything about the music? If I have to hear "*You're my hot thing and you make me sing when our love takes wing and we do our thing*" one more time, I'm going to end all of my problems but one and commit hari-kari."

"Dude, do you have your iPod with you?" Robb asked from his face plant position against the table top, the Fleb in his bio system having done almost as thorough a job as tequila.

"Of course, dude, always," said Johnny.

Robb pushed himself into an upright position with some difficulty, and opened a small panel in his chest, pulled out a wire, and handed the end of it to Johnny. "Plug it into this."

"Will it fit?" asked Johnny.

"Of course. Three point five millimeter mini-plug, universal standard," said Robb.

Johnny plugged in the iPod, and the screen on it lit up. "Sweet!" said Johnny, looking through the menu.

"In an emergency my head can be used as a six hundred watt boom box," said Robb.

"Play something good," said Steve.

"Yeah, yeah, I'll play something you old guys can enjoy too," said Johnny, and seconds later Robb/Bob Marley began singing about love and three little birds.

"Ahhh," I said, closing my eyes. "You're my hero, Robb. Now maybe I can relax."

"More Fleb!" shouted Larry.

"Or not," I said.

"*Hey, you!*" said a gruff, grumpy sounding voice.

I leaned back and listened to the music, hoping whoever it was was addressing someone else at the table other than me.

"*Hey, human!*" said the voice again, narrowing it down to one of three people.

I imagined birds and beaches and Nicole in a bikini.

"*Hey, Representative!*" said the voice.

"Crap," I said. I opened my eyes and found four to eight large blue and yellow spotted aliens, depending on how many heads were going to end up belonging to how many bodies, standing nearby looking angry. "Yeah?"

"You are the Representative of Earth, right?" said the obviously alpha male in the alien group. "That planet Bink was talking about on television that's full of eco terrorists? You know me and the boys here don't like eco terrorists."

"Is that a fact?" I said, closing my eyes again, and suddenly feeling like I was in a seedy bar on Tatooine.

"Yeah, it is. And we don't like him either," said another of gang.

"You'll have to be more specific than that," I said calmly, wondering what Bob Marley would do right about now.

"The one with the big mouth," said the alien.

"Oh, you mean Larry. We don't like him much, either," I said.

"Hey!" complained Larry.

"And we don't like robot trash, especially in our bar," said the alpha alien.

I opened first one eye, then the other, and stood up.

"Jake, please shit back down and try to ignore them," said Varcus. "They're Bufirts. Their race's favorite pash time is going around picking fights with other shpecies."

"It's okay; I got this," I said. "You know the metal dude's name you're talking about is Robb."

"He's a garbage disposal with feet," said the second alien.

Robb stood up quickly and wobbled angrily at the aliens. "You take that back or-" he said before falling over.

"Make me, circuit head," said the alien.

"Dude, I think now might be a good time to turn off your simulation program," said Johnny, under his breath.

"But you said-" began Robb from the floor.

"Just do it," said Johnny, eying the gang, who now looked even more unfriendly than before.

Robb made a mental maneuver and his head instantly cleared. He stood up and put Johnny's iPod inside his chest compartment for safe keeping and closed the door.

"Look guys. Let's all be real civilized here, shall we?" I said. "We don't want any trouble. Why don't you go sit back down and Larry'll buy you all a drink. Just listen to the music; like Bob's saying, we can all get along if we try."

"Yeah? I don't think so," said the alien.

I sighed. "Come on. Why not?"

"Because your music sucks too," said the alien.

I stared at him for a moment, then leaned in close and spoke slowly and quietly. "Be real careful now. You've insulted me, my species, one of my friends, and one of those guys you just kind of end up hanging around with no matter how hard you try not to; I could maybe live with all that. But that's Bob Marley singing. So choose your next words real carefully; what did you say about the music?"

The alien paused; although I didn't know it, he was feeling a little intimidated by the vibe of a being ten thousand years less removed than he was from killing in the wild to survive. "Well," he said a bit meekly, coming to the conclusion he may have underestimated his opponent, and that while some diplomacy wouldn't hurt him that much the being in front of him just might.

"Bob Marley sucks!" said a different alien in the back, who wasn't close enough to pick up on the sudden primeval aura hanging in the air.

"That's what I thought you said," I said, rearing back and sending a hard right fist into the chin of the alien in front of me, as Steve leapt from his chair to back me up for the umpteenth time. Robb bounced clear over the table and onto the head and shoulders of one of the aliens, little fists flying, while Johnny circled around trying to decide if the enemy's family jewels were likely to be where they were supposed to be.

Varcus sighed a big sigh. "Oh, hell," he said, and he got up, and picked up one of the aliens and tossed him halfway across the room.

Larry stood and puffed out his chest and chin, smiled a gigantic smile, and threw all four arms open wide. "Battle!" he cried happily, and launched himself into the fray.

Chapter Twenty Three

"Dude, I can't believe they threw us off the planet," said Johnny, as we cruised through space past the planet Trius of the Kador solar system.

"It's getting to be kind of a trend, isn't it?" said Steve.

"We sure showed those guys though, didn't we?" I said.

"It didn't hurt we had the purple Hercules on our side," said Steve, who was feeling a bit calmer this voyage now that he was a seasoned astronaut and Varcus had left the dome of the ship up.

"You were like a weed whacker, Robodude," said Johnny, reunited with his skateboard at last and fondling it fondly.

"It sort of helped my simulation circuits were off and I couldn't feel any pain," said Robb.

"Did you see that thing Larry did with his guy's left elbow and right ear? Ouch." I said.

Steve stretched. "Ouch is right, though. I'm pretty sore today."

"Yeah, a couple of them got in some good licks on me, too," I said. "But at least we don't all have hangovers on top of it. Those pills Varcus gave us did wonders. And I gotta say that was the nicest jail I've ever been in."

"It was a lot better than the one I was in on Earth the night before," said Robb, who was now an almost seasoned enough ex-con to start composing Johnny Cash songs.

A door opened and Varcus walked into the room. "Jake, we need to talk."

"Yeah, I know. I'm sorry about last night," I said.

"Last night? Oh that; don't worry about it. They had it coming," said Varcus.

"You're not mad?" asked Steve.

"No, why should I be?" said Varcus.

"Then you didn't get into any trouble for it?" I asked.

"Not yet. It'll be coming sooner or later though, so at least I've got something to look forward to," said Varcus.

"I didn't hear. Did they ban you from Kador for a year, too?" I said.

"Again not yet, mostly because I'm a government official of sorts," said Varcus. "They banned Larry of course, but then they do that about once a year anyway."

"Good old Larry," I said, having managed to grow a bit fonder of him now that we had bonded in the fire of combat.

"Well, good old Larry is what I wanted to talk to you about," said Varcus. "I just got off the phone with Verice, my ancestral half-cousin three hundred and seventy-eight times removed on my mother's side. She cocktails in the lounge on space station Robeela, and she said Larry was there last week and told her some very interesting things before they threw him off the station. Do you guys know for instance why he wants to move you to Aurora?"

"So he'll finally have some friends?" suggested Steve.

"No, but that's a good guess," said Varcus.

"I thought it was because he wanted pizza," I said.

"You're right; he does. In fact he wants it so bad he's bringing you to the planet just so he can open a pizza parlor," said Varcus. "A really *big* pizza parlor."

"Like, how big?" I said.

"Big enough to serve the entire galaxy," said Varcus.

"That's pretty big," I agreed.

"Yes. It will cover a good portion of the planet. Larry plans to use the same displacement technology we use on our space ships to transport piping hot pizzas to hungry aliens everywhere," said Varcus. "And he's going to use your people to grow the ingredients and bake them. He hopes to make a bundle."

"And if we get to Aurora and simply refuse to go along with his evil plan?" I said.

"Then he can make you do what he wants by pointing a ray or two at you," said Varcus.

"What, you guys have a ray that'll turn us all into Domino's zombies?" asked Steve.

"No, but Larry could use one that makes you all vulnerable to suggestions," said Varcus. "The practice is definitely frowned upon, but Aurora is a privately owned planet so no one could interfere."

"And you're sure about all this?" I said.

"I'm afraid so," said Varcus. "He even offered to bring Verice back to his ship and show her his pizza pie charts."

"Boy, if that isn't the oldest line in the book," I said. "He better hope he's not around when I get back to Earth."

A ship's buzzer sounded three times. "Which will be in just a couple of moments," said Varcus. "I have to get back to the bridge and land us," he said, and left the room.

"So what are you going to do?" said Steve.

"What am I going to do?" I said. "Let's just say pizza guy and me are going to have a nice little chat when we get back."

Chapter Twenty Four

I stepped out of Varcus' ship and onto the ramp, and a sea of flashbulbs went off in my face. I blinked and waited for the spots to clear out of my eyes, then opened them and found a crowd of aliens of all sizes, shapes, and colors milling about the pasture and yard. I stared at them in disbelief for a moment, then walked down the ramp followed by Steve, who pushed his way through the crowd towards the house, anxious to see his new bride.

A pudgy creature wearing a flowered shirt and a hat with a feather in it walked up and held up a picture, comparing it to me. "This is him! This is the Representative," he said, and another wave of flashes popped off.

"Ooh! The Representative!" said a tall blue alien with three eyes.

"Take my picture with it!" said a yellow and red spotted creature with wings.

A slimy looking alien covered in moving fungus held out an equally slimy looking book. "Can I have your autograph?"

"What the hell is going on here?" I said. "Who are all you things, uh, people?"

"Oh, sorry," said the pudgy alien. "Din Weeber. Sun Planet tours," he said, then pointed to a gaudy looking ship resembling a tour bus painted with stars, comets, and planets, that was parked in the street.

"What are you all doing here?" I asked.

"Touring your planet. Seeing you and your people in their natural habitat before you're not in it anymore," explained Din.

"This is not good. Cynthia is not going to like this," I said.

"Look, mammal excretions," said a three legged alien. "Take a picture of me with them."

"Remember, folks, it's against interstellar customs regulations to remove anything from an undeveloped planet, doomed inhabitants or otherwise," said Din, into an electronic megaphone.

A dignified voice came from behind me. "Pardon me, but you are the Representative aren't you?"

I turned and found a green, eight foot tall plant covered in little orange colored blossoms addressing me. "That's what everyone keeps telling me," I said, at the point now where nothing came as a shock anymore.

"If you have a moment I would like to talk to you about the future of the plant life here on Earth," said the creature. "I know as a mammal you probably overlook the well being of vegetation, but if you could just hear me out."

"Look, I don't have time for this," I said. "The only plant I give a hoot about is the potted fern back in my living room, and he's perfectly safe."

"If you really cared about him you would set him free so he could frolic in the wild," said the plant.

"I don't think he's much into frolicking, but I'll ask him the next chance I get," I said, looking around for someplace else to be. "Now beat it before I go looking for Steve's weed whacker."

The plant creature managed to look scared and moved quickly off.

"Quite a mess, isn't it?" asked Varcus, who had come out of the ship to see what he could do to help.

"What is that thing, anyway?" I said, pointing at the plant, who was bending down to shake hands with a not so innocent dandelion.

"A Chrysanthaman," said Varcus. "Pollinated, too. He'll be bearing fruit in a few weeks."

"That's probably all I want to know about that," I said. I looked over and saw that Larry's ship was back, and spying him near it talking to two curvaceous orange tourists, stomped towards him, Varcus following. "Hey, Larry! I want to talk to you!"

The two identically attractive tangerine creatures moved off. "I hope this is important," Larry said sadly, watching them leave. "You chased off the twins."

"They're all twins, you moron," said Varcus.

"What do you mean?" said Larry.

"Go to Olandal some time. It's inhabitants are all identical," said Varcus.

Larry considered this. "That could be most fun," he said thoughtfully.

"Including the males and females," said Varcus. "They're impossible to tell apart, even for Olandals."

"Hm; I'll have to consider that further. The potential for extremely embarrassing situations might outweigh the potential for quintuple horizontal mamboing," said Larry. "Anyway, what did you want, Jake? I suppose since Varcus moves you tomorrow morning you're finally ready to take me up on my gallant offer?"

"You suppose wrong," I snapped. "Varcus passed on some information from one of his sources, and I can tell you right now there's no way the human race is going to spend eternity tossing pizza dough for you."

Larry thought for a moment. "Verice! I hate how every Vandorian is related."

"Yes we are, and stop hitting on my cousins," said Varcus.

"I can't help it. I have a weakness for tall, dark, violet women," said Larry.

"You know, you have some nerve trying to trick these people," said Varcus.

"Me? At least I'm not moving them to some hole and giving their home to a race of annoying little twerps," said Larry.

"What?!" I said.

"Um-" said Varcus. "Perhaps I should explain."

"Perhaps you should. Do you mean to tell me you have someone else waiting to move onto the Earth?" I said.

"Yes; I admit I do. The Kapaloo. Their world is doomed, you see," said Varcus.

"Why should they get our home just because their own planet is doomed?" I said.

"Because unlike your people, they're not the ones who doomed it," said Varcus.

Nicole walked up to us. "Welcome home, Jake. What's going on?"

"The purple people mover here gave our planet to another species and didn't think it was important enough to tell us," I said.

"You still have Aurora to fall back on," said Larry. "Sandy beaches, champagne wishes, and caviar dreams."

"And spending the rest of my life on the phone asking if some space gerbil wants thin or thick crust? No thank you," I said.

A short, bookworm looking little alien with spectacles tugged on my shirt hem. "Can I have a lock of your hair, mister alien?"

203

"Hey! No DNA samples!" said Din, and he rushed over and guided the creature away.

"But I just wanted to clone him when I got home," protested the nerdling.

"I can't take much more of this," I said.

Steve came out of the house with a cell phone in his hand and shouted across the yard. "Hey, Jake!"

"Hey, what?!" I shouted back.

"The President is on the phone," said Steve.

"Which one?" I said.

"*The* one," said Steve.

"Oh, that one," I said. "About time! Maybe I'm finally gonna get some help around here."

"I don't think so," said Steve. "He and the First Lady are packing and they want to know if they should bring their bathing suits."

"That does it!" I said, exasperated. "I've had it. I didn't ask for any of this, and I'm done dealing with it. Move us, keep us here, make us slice pepperoni, I don't care anymore!" I looked around, then walked off towards the back of the property.

"Jake, where are you going?" asked Nicole.

"Away," I said without turning, not really knowing where I was headed.

"You can't walk off the planet, you know," said Larry, shouting after me.

Chapter Twenty Five

I sat on a grassy hill on the edge of a small bluff that overlooked the farm. It was near sunset, the sky turning every shade of red and gold it could think of. Insects and little dandelion puffs floated around me in the light evening breeze. I stared out into the distance at my surroundings, my knees up and my arms resting upon them.

"There you are," said Nicole, as she came up beside me. "I've been looking everywhere for you."

"Yep. Here I am," I said, still gazing off into the distance.

"We were all worried about you," she said.

"Just needed to be by myself for a while," I said.

"Would you like me to leave?" asked Nicole.

I finally looked up at her. "No; have a seat," I said, and she sat down next to me. "The alien paparazzi still down at the farm?"

"Nope. Cynthia came out on the porch with a shotgun and fired off a couple of warning shots, and they all cleared out in a hurry," said Nicole.

"That's my girl. I'm beginning to understand what Steve sees in her," I said.

"So what happened down there?" Nicole asked.

"I don't know. All of a sudden it really hit me what was going on, I guess," I said.

"I suppose it's not very fair you having to deal with all this," said Nicole.

"That's just the thing though," I said. "I've been thinking about it, and it is fair."

"What do you mean?" said Nicole.

"I mean I'm just as guilty as the next civilized human when it comes to the planet's environment," I said. "It would be unfair if it was a pygmy from some lost tribe that had been served; he'd wonder what the hell he'd done to deserve it. But I'm not exactly mister green jeans myself, you know. Sure, I throw a can in the recycle bin from time to time. But other than that it's all about whatever works for me. I just want to crank up the air conditioning in my apartment, hop in a taxi, go a few blocks, then get out and buy a bunch of stuff and consume. Maybe stop on the way home and get a burger made from an ecologically unfriendly, methane venting cow. But is any of that worth losing all of this?" I said, pointing at the vista all around us. "It's beautiful, isn't it?"

"Yes it is," said Nicole.

"You know, I've never stopped and looked at it before; nature, I mean. Not that I've been knee deep in it most of my life. But it's never even occurred to me that I should care about it. I love my city; I really do. But would I love it any less if it weren't such a strain on the planet? Would it kill me to walk a few blocks instead of grabbing a cab? We're just this fly speck in the history of the Earth, and our biggest legacy isn't going to be what a wonderful world we created. Instead it's going to be how we changed the planet itself for the worse. The more I think about it, the more I wonder if we shouldn't just go along quietly to Gork and give the poor Earth a break. At least we'd be saving the Pakaloons," I said. "Not that we have much choice in the matter anyway."

"You know, Jake, in our defense, we have made life better. Can you imagine how harsh living was a thousand years ago?" said Nicole.

"I know. We just didn't know when to stop," I said.

"I guess maybe you're right," said Nicole.

There was a long, quiet moment as we sat soaking up our surroundings.

"We should be getting back soon," said Nicole finally.

"Yeah. But not quite yet," I said.

"Okay. Not yet," said Nicole, and she leaned over and put her head on my shoulder.

Chapter Twenty Six

It was moving day, and we were all scrambling to get ready.

"Steve!" shouted Cynthia. "Would you get in here? You're going to miss it."

"I think this is one flight you can't miss," said Nicole.

Steve rushed into the living room holding up a box of matches, before putting them into his backpack. "Suddenly remembered watching *"Cast Away"* with Tom Hanks," he said. "I'm not very good at rubbing sticks together."

"Yeah, I get the feeling I'm going to regret being the only person in America who didn't watch Survivor," I said. I looked around the room; "So where do you guys think? Right here okay?"

Steve looked up. "I'm thinking outside. I don't know how this is gonna work, but I really don't want to go up through the roof if I don't have to."

"Good point. Outside it is," I said.

The four of us picked up our bags and walked outside, then went over to an open area of grass devoid of trees, near the two space ships. Larry, who was sitting in a chair outside of his ship, shouted, "Are you sure you don't want to change your minds? Making pizza is a noble profession, and you would all make good tips."

"No thanks. I might get used to being a slave, but I'd get so sick and tired of pizza that I'd never want to eat it again, and that I couldn't live with," I shouted back.

"In my opinion you're not looking at the big picture, but then again the picture in this case is quite humongous so perhaps it will take your eyes some time to critique it all," said Larry. "I'll stop in and visit you on Gork, and maybe by then you'll have finished your viewing."

"You do that," I said, knowing I probably couldn't stop him from coming if I wanted to.

"Do you think this is going to hurt?" asked Nicole.

"Naw," I said. "They're just going to suck us off the planet into ships miles away up in space, probably tearing every molecule in our bodies apart before slamming them all back together again. Why should it hurt?"

"Thanks for making me feel better," said Nicole.

"Don't mention it," I said.

We waited for a while in the midst of yet another in the string of beautiful days the Earth had kicked out lately, as if it was showing everyone what they were going to be missing from now on.

"I'm going to miss all this," said Steve, reading the Earth's message loud and clear.

"Me too," I said.

"Maybe Gork won't be as bad as it sounds," said Nicole.

"Maybe," I said. "Or maybe it will be a lot worse and they just didn't want to scare us."

"You know, you're just a ray of sunshine today," said Nicole.

Everyone stood holding their bags and waiting some more, this more seeming quite long. "Does anyone have a watch?" asked Cynthia finally. "My arms are getting tired."

"No," said Nicole and I together.

"I didn't see the point either with the shorter days on Gork," said Steve. " I'd have to reset the thing every nine hours."

We waited a short bit longer.

"Are we there-" I began, but was interrupted as the four of us disappeared from the Earth, accompanied by strange, wet, popping sounds, like a big finger coming out of a mouth.

We reappeared inside a transport ship with four more popping sounds, followed very quickly by hundreds of other people in an avalanche of wet pops. Everyone was squeezed together in the dull, gray, dingy hold, which was lit by strips of yellow lighting running around the ceiling where it met with the walls.

"-yet?" I finished.

"Welcome to transport ship 2738-B," said a robotic sounding voice over a loud speaker. *"Please remain standing for the duration of the trip."*

"And I thought coach was bad," said Nicole. "This is going to be a long flight."

"Thank you for your cooperation," said the voice a second or so later. *"And welcome to Gork."*

"You were saying?" I said, unsurprised and well versed in space travel times.

"We can't be there al-" began Nicole, before vanishing in a pop.

"-ready," said Nicole, as she reappeared on the surface of Gork alongside Steve, Cynthia, and I, as other people from the Annandale area arrived in the distance in a barrage of pops.

I dropped my bags and looked around me.

"Man, we are so doomed," said Steve.

"For once I agree with you," I said.

It was a dark place. The sky was filled with sickly green and yellow swirling clouds, while the ground was made up of brown, black, and gray dirt and rock. Black wooded trees with dark leaves grew scattered about. Yellow scrub bushes stuck out of the ground and orange moss grew on many of the stones. Odd noises seemed to come from everywhere, some like animals or birds, but others indefinable. The wind made an annoying off key whistling sound.

Everyone began to sweat immediately in the intense heat as Nicole snapped a picture of the planet. "I don't know," she said. "It could be worse. Couldn't it?"

"Only if we were dead already, and even that might be an improvement," said Steve, just seconds before a snarling, growling sound came from somewhere on the ground behind him.

Steve froze, and I looked down to see what was making the noise that had sent a chill down my spine in the one hundred degree plus heat. "Uh, Steve? Did you mean what you said about death possibly being an improvement?" I said.

"What is that, Jake?" asked Steve, doing his best to imitate a rock.

"If I had to name it, I'd call it fangs with feet," I said.

"What should I do?" said Steve.

"Run like hell," I said.

Steve looked down behind him and yelped, then dropped his bags and took off running as fast as he could. The ugly, three foot long creature with a single eye and wide mouthful of teeth above six legs chased after him, snarling as it went.

"Steve!" shrieked Cynthia, dropping her belongings too and running after them.

"Well, they'll be busy for a while," I said. "Damn it's hot," I added, wiping the sweat off my brow.

"The film said it was going to be hot," said Nicole.

"No, they said it was going to be hot," I said. "This isn't hot. I've been in hot before, and this makes hot seem cool. I'm going to have to come up a new word for this hot."

Nicole saw something and pointed. "What are those things?" she asked, taking a picture.

I looked over at the tree which Nicole was pointing. at. In it sat two very large bird like creatures, about five feet or so tall. They looked almost like giant vultures, but had a single eye and ratty fur instead of feathers. The beasts gazed down at the people below them with interest.

"I don't know, but I hope they don't decide to make us part of the local food chain," I said.

A small silver robot with spindly arms and a TV screen for a face flew up to us. "Greetings, and welcome to Gork," it said, the words simultaneously scrolling across its screen. "I am an orientation bot. Please pick out a shelter to live in. A shower and restroom facility is located in the center of your designated area, alongside a mess hall where delicious food and water can be found. Sustenance will be provided for six Gorkian months;

after that you are on your own. Do you have any questions?"

"I do," said Nicole. "Where are all the other humans? I just see the same townspeople I saw in Annandale."

"That is because your species has been placed on Gork in as close a relation as possible to where you were picked up on Earth. It would appear you came from a sparsely populated area," explained the robot.

"So a few hundred miles to the east there are about ten million people crammed closely together?" I said.

"If you mean the citizens of the Chicago and Milwaukee metropolitan area, then yes," said the robot.

"We lucked out there," I said. "I loved Chicago, but I don't need to be packed together like sardines with all those people, on a planet with no skyscrapers to hold us all vertically."

"I'll say," said Nicole.

The robot buzzed off to greet other arrivals.

"You know, I feel kind of light," said Nicole, moving up and down on her heels and toes.

"Me too; like I have a new pair of sneaks on," I said. I jumped up and down a little and liked what I felt, then crouched, and jumped as high as I could. To my surprise I shot up about ten feet off the ground, then came back down, landing a bit clumsily. "That was crazy," I said. "The gravity must be lower here. Look, I can be like Mike."

I spent the next few minutes having a great time bouncing merrily around the area imitating Michael Jordan, as Nicole watched. Finally she yawned and said "Well, this is fun but I'm going to go check out the shelters."

I landed reluctantly back down on the surface. "Wait, I'll go with you."

We managed to pick up our and Steve and Cynthia's bags, and lugged them over to the nearest shelter. It was an institutional green, plastic looking building which was shaped more or less like a cheap, small house. I knocked on a wall to test it, then Nicole opened the door and we went inside. The room we entered was a common area with doors leading off to other rooms. Block shaped chairs, benches and tables were molded into the floor. Light filtered in through screened windows.

"I wish I would have brought some magazines with me," I said, looking the room over. "I'm gonna need something to read if I'm going to live in a giant porta-potty." I peeked into one of the four side rooms, which turned out to be a sleeping area with a single molded bed, complete with foam mattress, and tossed my bags inside. I explored some more and found another room with two such beds, and put Steve and Cynthia's luggage into it. "This setup is really going to put a cramp in the newlywed's style. Hey, you want to stay here, too?"

"Why, Jake; are you asking me to move in with you?" asked Nicole, batting her eyelashes at him.

"I'm asking you to grab one of those last two rooms before some weirdo takes them," I said.

"I don't know," said Nicole thoughtfully. "I should probably try and find my parents."

"You sure you want to walk halfway across an alien planet to New Milwaukee?" I said.

"Good point," said Nicole, and she put her things into one of the rooms.

"Cool. Now we just have to find one more roomie," I said.

Nicole looked around her. "It's not much, but I guess it'll keep us dry."

A tapping noise came on the roof of our new home, followed quickly by two, then three, then eight more. They multiplied quickly and noisily on the hard plastic-like surface, growing louder and louder, until we had to yell to at one another to hear.

"What the hell is that?" I shouted, hands over my ears.

"I think it's rain." Nicole yelled back.

"I'd rather be wet than deaf. Come on," I said, heading towards the door.

We rushed outside and almost ran into Johnny, who was carrying a couple of huge bags and his skateboard. "Repman! Dude, are you guys living in there?"

"Um..." I said.

"Cool, dude. I was looking for a place to live. My mom said it was a good time for me to finally move out of her house. You've got space, don't ya?" said Johnny.

"Well, yeah but-" I said.

"You don't mind, do you?" Johnny asked Nicole.

"Well..." said Nicole.

"Sweet. I'll just put my stuff inside," said Johnny, before going through the door.

We stood looking at one another in the rain as if the other should have done something about the new wrinkle in our housing situation, but were soon distracted by a sudden assault on our olfactory senses.

"What the hell is that smell?" I asked.

"I don't know, but it's awful," said Nicole, crinkling her nose.

I sniffed all around me, then smelled Nicole, and recoiled in disgust. "Damn! What perfume are you wearing, essence of boiled cabbage?"

Nicole smelled herself. "Ugh. It's not me, it's the rain."

I caught some in my hand, took a whiff, and almost gagged. "Dats just great," I said, holding my nose shut.

Steve came running up and stopped, bending over and putting his hands on his knees to rest, fully out of breath.

"You got away from that thing, huh? Still got all your body parts?" I said.

Steve nodded and I looked around.

"Hey, where's Cynthia?" I asked. "That creature didn't-"

"No, she's fine," panted Steve. "She ducked into the mess hall when the rain started. Are we all living in there?" he asked, pointing at the shelter.

"Yeah, we put your bags inside," I said.

"Thanks, buddy," said Steve, finally able to stand up.

A loud rolling sound came from inside the shelter.

"What's that noise?" asked Steve.

"That would be your new roommate skateboarding around the living room," said Nicole.

"Johnny's in there? Who said he could live with us?" asked Steve.

Nicole and I pointed at one another.

"What the hell. No point in going half-assed about it, I guess; might as well be totally miserable," said

Steve. "Come on, let's get out of this rain. I'll show you the way to the mess hall."

The three of us headed towards a very large plastic building in the center of all the shelters. Steve opened the door for Nicole and she went inside.

"You know a few days of this place and I'll be ready to go extinct," said Steve.

"I'll be right behind you," I said.

"You think that's what happened to the dinosaurs?" said Steve.

"What, the planet annoyed them to death? I don't think the Earth was ever this bad, even the parts without cable. Come on, let's see what's for lunch," I said, and slapped Steve on the back as we went inside.

It was soon night, the dim, gloomy, Gorkian sky having quickly faded into a dark, gloomy, starless veil. We sat together on a circle of large rocks around a campfire Steve had built with his matches.

"Well, we survived our first day on Gork," said Steve.

"We've been here five hours," I said.

"Still," said Steve.

"Dinner like totally sucked didn't it?" said Johnny.

"It might be a little more palatable if it didn't come out of a big vat labeled human food," said Nicole.

"That was kind of a turn off," I said. "And I hope the name didn't mean what it tasted like it meant."

"Well, I have a surprise for everyone," said Steve. He reached behind him and got his backpack, and pulled out a box of graham crackers, a bag of marshmallows, and a bag of mini Hershey bars. "Ta-da!"

"Steve! You remembered the smores this time!" I said.

"I thought we might all need a treat on our first night," said Steve. He grabbed some sticks he'd collected and handed them out, then passed around the marshmallows. Soon everyone was roasting them over the fire, smiling at a simple Earth pleasure.

"Thanks, Steve," said Johnny.

"Yeah, good thinking," I said. "All we need now is a case of cold beer," I said.

"I'll see what I can do, bro," said Johnny.

"Right. What are you gonna do, skateboard down to the local liquor store?" said Steve.

"Don't worry man, I got it covered," said Johnny.

"Good. Then stop at McDonald's on the way back and pick up some Big Macs," I said.

"Duuuuudes," said Johnny, hurt at the lack of confidence.

We sat quietly for a while, munching and thinking.

"I miss my cows," said Cynthia.

"I miss the house," said Steve.

"I miss Earth air," said Nicole.

"This is like Earth air," I said. "Ever been to L.A.?"

There was a silent pause, then Nicole said, "We're never going to see it again, are we? Earth, that is."

"Oh, I don't know. Never is a long time," I said. "Things you don't expect happen."

"They certainly do," said Steve.

Chapter Twenty Seven (And two Gorkian weeks later)

Tommy stood on the mound and shook off the sign from Steve. Then he shook it off again. And again. And again.

"Would you just pitch it already? It's underhand softball for crying out loud!" said Steve.

"Just trying to add a little drama," said Tommy.

"Squatting here in this heat is drama enough," said Steve.

Tommy went into his windup and tossed the softball and it arced gracefully towards home plate, until my bat intercepted it and sent it sailing high into the angry Gorkian sky and far off into the distance.

"Dammit, Jake!" complained Craig, who was playing first base.

"Oops! My bad," I said.

"Who's gonna go get it this time?" asked Steve. A low, menacing growl came from behind him, and he sighed. "Never mind; I got it," he said, and tossed his glove to me, then took off running in the direction the ball had gone, Fangfeet right on his heels for the fourteenth day in a row.

"Hey, Jake," said Tommy, pointing behind me. I turned and found Varcus standing nearby with a five foot tall, very thin, furry red alien. The being had long, pointy ears, and resembled an ugly kangaroo.

"Varcus! What are you doing here? Come to see if we messed up Gork yet?" I said. "Although I don't know how you'd be able to tell."

"Hello, Jake. No, I'm here because I need to talk to you," said Varcus.

I dropped my bat and Steve's glove on the ground and walked over. "Okay. We have to wait for the ball to come back anyway; I keep forgetting to lighten up on my swing in this low gravity."

"This is Qwas. He's one of the Kapaloos, the race that was moving to the Earth," said Varcus.

"Jake Williams, Representative," I said, putting out my hand to shake, but Qwas looked at it as if I'd offered him a decaying fish.

"Sorry, I make it a point to avoid contact with primitive alien creatures," said Qwas, in an annoying, nasally voice. "You never know where they've been."

"Suit yourself," I said. "Let's head over to my office."

We walked away from our makeshift baseball field and towards a large gas grill, where Mark was cooking. A table next to him was covered with bowls filled with beans, chips, and dips. "How do you want your steak done, Jake?" he asked.

"Medium rare," I said.

"You got it. Hello, Varcus," said Mark.

Varcus looked puzzled. "You have steaks?"

I grabbed a handful of chips and started munching on them. "Yeah; someone must have brought 'um with them from the Earth."

"And the grill?" asked Varcus.

"I guess someone brought that too," I said.

Varcus looked unconvinced but said nothing, and we continued walking until we came to a green metal cooler under a big beach umbrella. I opened the cooler and pulled a frosty bottle out of the ice. "You guys want a cold beer?"

"No!" said Varcus irritably.

"Ack! Certainly not," said Qwas.

I shrugged and opened the bottle, and took a long drink. "Ah," I said. "You guys don't know what you're missing. Nothing like a frosty brew on a fine Gorkian day."

"Alright, Jake, what's going on?" said Varcus.

"What do you mean?" I said innocently.

"You know exactly what I mean!" said Varcus. "Where'd all this stuff come from? The grill, steaks, beer...and ice? Where in Kelgrin did you get manage to find ice on this planet? And don't tell me somebody brought it."

"How else would we get it?" I asked. "Have you seen many humans cruising around out there in space?"

"Well, no, I haven't, but-" said Varcus.

"Then I guess we must have brought everything with us," I said.

"It's Larry, isn't it? I bet these are all bribes from him, aren't they?" said Varcus.

"No, but if they were I'd gladly accept them; we need all the help we can get," I said. "Larry is around here somewhere though, peddling a petition to try and get me to move everyone to Aurora. I told him I'd consider it if he got four billion signatures."

"Four *billion*?" said Varcus.

"Yeah, I figure it should keep him out of my hair for a few days at least," I said.

"Ola, Varcus dude!" said Johnny, as he walked by. "How's my main metal man Robb Ott?"

"More rebellious than ever," said Varcus. "Some day I'd like to know what you did to him."

"Just played him some tunes," said Johnny.

"I had no idea Earth music was so dangerous," said Varcus.

"Only when it's done right," said Johnny.

"How's the skate park coming, Johnny?" I asked.

"Almost done, dude. The cement should be dry by tomorrow," said Johnny.

"Sweeeeeet," I said.

Johnny waved goodbye and wandered off to do whatever it was he did every day.

"Cement?" said Varcus. "I suppose you're going to tell me someone brought that, too."

I did my best innocent look again, and Varcus sighed.

"Fine; be that way. But I will get to the bottom of it," said Varcus.

"You do that," I said.

Varcus opened his mouth to say something, but stopped and looked off to his left, puzzled. "Jake, who are all those people?"

I looked over and found a group of miserable, sweaty looking humans staring angrily back at me.

"Oh them. Just ignore 'em; I do," I said.

"But who are they?" asked Varcus.

"They're my fan club from New Glenbrook," I said. "They blame me for this whole Gork thing, but since you still have that pacifist ray aimed at us they can't do anything about it. So they just drop by every day and give me dirty looks."

"Oh my," said Varcus.

"I'm getting used to it. But I am a little worried what's going to happen when you turn the thing off," I said. "So how are you Poopaloos liking the Earth? Did you re-carve Mount Rushmore yet?"

"Kapaloos. And you filthy beings should be ashamed of yourselves," said Qwas. "A nice planet like that and you refused to take care of it."

"Hey, you want to tone down the attitude a bit, or are you looking to take part in an intergalactic incident right here and now?" I said.

"What kind of intergalactic incident?" said Qwas.

"The kind where I reach out and yank on those stupid looking ears of yours so hard they'll be dragging on the ground," I said. For some reason I'd found that since going to Kador I seemed to be unaffected by the pacifist ray, and was more than ready right now to make some kangaroo steaks.

"Ack!" said Qwas.

"Boys..." said Varcus.

Steve came jogging up, totally out of breath but in the best shape of his life by now.

"Larry was right; they are annoying little twerps," I said.

"Huh?" said Steve, panting.

"Did you get the ball?" I asked.

"Yes and no. I found it and grabbed it on the run while that little s.o.b. was chasing me, then ran back towards the field. I tried to throw the ball to Mark, but I forgot about the gravity and it sailed off over his head," explained Steve. "Funny thing is, Fangfeet took off after it."

"Can we get back to what I came here to talk to you about?" said Varcus "We have a bit of a problem."

227

"We? In case you haven't noticed *we* already have a problem of our own, so I'm not sure we want anything to do with this new one of yours," I said. "But go ahead and pile some more on us."

"When the Kapaloo advance team came down to check out the Earth, they began sneezing and all their hair fell out," said Varcus. "And if there's one thing you don't want to see it's naked, hairless, Kapaloos. No offense."

"Ack!" said Qwas.

"Wow, I feel real sorry for them," I dead-panned. "So what's wrong? Are they allergic to strawberries or something?"

"No, to the sky," said Varcus.

"The sky? What, you mean like oxygen, nitrogen, that kind of thing?" asked Steve.

"No, the color," said Varcus.

"Come again," I said.

"It turns out the Kapaloo are allergic to the color blue, at least in large quantities or close proximity," said Varcus. "There's no blue on their home world; they can't even see it. The Earth sky just looked blank to them. We had a devil of a time trying to figure out what was wrong with them."

"That's the stupidest thing I've ever heard, and I've heard some whoppers in the last couple of weeks," I said. "Hey, Steve, give me your shirt."

Steve peeled off his light blue, sweat drenched tee shirt and tossed it to me.

"This is definitely all bull shit," I said. I held the shirt out very close to Qwas, and the creature sneezed extremely hard, his fur flying off in every direction.

"Okay, maybe not," I said.

Qwas stood and tried to cover himself. "That's just perfect," he said irritably.

"And I was sure you couldn't get any uglier," I said.

"Now do you believe me?" said Varcus.

I held the shirt to my nose and sniffed it. "Phew! I don't know, Steve's deodorant gave out about a week ago, I think. If I had to smell his shirt too many times my hair would probably fall out, too."

"Trust me, it's the color," said Varcus.

"So can't you just give them all sunglasses or something?" I said.

"It wouldn't help. The sky would still be there," said Varcus.

"Looks like you do have a problem. Wish I could help," I said.

"Glad to hear you say that, Jake," said Varcus.

"Sorry, I bet you thought I meant that," I said.

Fangfeet came jogging up to Steve, the softball lodged firmly between his chompers. He deposited it at Steve's feet and stood growling at him, jaws open, mouth drooling, and tail wagging. Steve gingerly reached out and picked up the slimy, mutilated remains of the ball and threw it way off into the distance, and Fangfeet snarled happily and charged off after it.

"What do you know; all this time he just wanted to play," said Steve.

"Look, this will help you and your people too, Jake," said Varcus. "Since there's no blue to be found anywhere on Gork, we've decided to move the Kapaloos here instead."

"So are you putting us back on Earth then?" I asked hopefully.

"No, but we can move you to Dacoola Five. It's a bit nicer than Gork, more temperate. A class C planet; Gork is a D. It will still be difficult, but your people will have a much better chance of survival there."

"That's great news, isn't it, Jake?" said Steve, then when I didn't respond, said, "Jake?" again.

"Uh-uh," I said.

"Uh-uh? Uh-uh as in it's not great news?" said Steve.

"Uh-uh. Uh-uh as in I think we'll just stay right here," I said.

"Are you crazy?" said Steve. "This planet is a dump. Anywhere is better than here."

"I don't know, I kind of like it. Besides, Johnny just finished his skateboard park," I said.

"Look, it's not like you have a lot of say in the matter," said Varcus.

"Don't I? I'm still the Representative right? We haven't messed up Gork yet, have we?" I said.

"Well, yes and yes but..." said Varcus.

"Then I'm thinking you can't move us unless I say it's alright, and we can stay put here if we want to," I said.

"Yes but *we* don't want to," said Steve.

Nicole and Larry came walking up to us, Nicole looking for some back up in the face of yet another of Larry's advances. "What's going on?" she asked.

"Jake's finally gone insane in the heat," said Steve. Nicole leaned close to him and he quietly brought her up to speed.

"You're being difficult for no good reason, Jake. The Kapaloo can't survive on Earth, and their home world will soon be uninhabitable," said Varcus.

"Then I guess they're screwed aren't they? Unless you want to put us back on the Earth," I said.

"You know I can't do that," said Varcus.

"This is all your fault!" screeched Qwas shrilly.

"My fault?" said Varcus.

"You're the one who sold us that planet," said Qwas.

"Sold it? You didn't mention any money being involved. No wonder you were so anxious to move us," I said.

"I didn't make any profit from it," said Varcus. "Most of the money went to pay for moving all of you around, and the rest went into the planetary protection fund."

"It doesn't matter! You sold us a planet we can't live on!" complained Qwas.

"I am sorry, but you passed all the compatibility tests and signed the papers," said Varcus.

"You should have been more thorough!" said Qwas.

"There's nothing I can do now," said Varcus.

"You know there is, Varcus," I said. "We'll be glad to hand Gork over to you and the Krapaloons. Just put us back where we belong."

"You belong here. Or on some other planet. But not on Earth; not anymore," said Varcus.

"I guess you're in a tight spot then, aren't you?" I said. "Because it looks like they aren't too happy."

"I'd sue you if I was them," said Larry.

"Ack! We would too, but we ate all our lawyers," said Qwas.

"We've got some we could loan you if you'd promise not to eat them," I said.

"You have lawyers?" said Qwas.

"Thousands upon thousands of them," I said. "In fact, there's one right here!" I said, pointing at Steve and tossing his shirt to him. "Put your clothes back on and try to look lawyerly."

"And they would file suit for us?" asked Qwas.

"Now wait a minute!" said Varcus.

"Steve and I would love to; it's what we do," I said.

"Actually, under interstellar law each plaintiff can have a separate lawyer file a grievance," said Larry.

"One for each lawyer?" I said. "What do we have, Steve? About a million attorneys?"

"Probably in the U.S. alone," said Steve.

"You can't do this!" said Varcus.

"Why not?" I said.

"Because...because...because for one thing, neither you nor the Kapaloos have interstellar travel. You won't even be able to physically file!" said Varcus.

"I have interstellar travel. And I'll be glad to do it for them," said Larry.

"Why would you want to do something like that?" said Varcus.

"In exchange for free pizza," said Larry. "And because I know it would irritate you."

Varcus sighed. "Fine; I'll refund the Kapaloo's money. But you humans are staying put!"

"We don't want the money! It won't help us if we're burned to cinders," said Qwas. "We need a planet to live on. Give them back the Earth so we can have Gork!'

"You heard the bald guy," I said. "Better do as he says, or we'll have you stuck in court for the next ten thousand years. You'll have to time travel forward just to have the sun shine on your arse again."

Varcus stared angrily at me, and I stared confidently back.

"Well? What's it going to be, Varcus?" I said.

"Give me a moment. I need to make a call," said Varcus sourly.

"Take your time," I said.

Varcus walked some distance away, got out his PED, and was soon speaking into it.

"Do you think this is going to work, Jake?" asked Nicole.

"It does seem kind of risky," said Steve.

"Look, stop worrying; I have 'em right where I want 'em," I said, believing just that. "It's just like a divorce. They want the condo in Miami but they're not going to get it unless they give us the cabin in Vale."

"Can't we have the condo in Miami instead?" asked Larry. "I need to work on my tan."

"The point is, option one, they'll give us back the Earth and we'll all be as happy as can be. Or option two, they'll force us to move to this other planet Varcus was talking about, and we'll at least be happier than we are now. Or option three, they'll leave us here on Gork and we'll be totally miserable, but hey, that's what we were to begin with," I said. "I mean, what's the worst that can happen?"

"I hope you're right," said Nicole.

Varcus put the PED away and came back over.

"So?" I said.

"So they're immediately convening an emergency session of the Galactic Council," said Varcus. "And then there will be a vote on the matter."

"To decide if we stay here or go back to Earth?" asked Nicole.

"Yes," said Varcus.

"Good," I said.

"Or if they exterminate you to get you out of the way of the Kapaloo," said Varcus.

"I guess you forgot to mention option four in your famous *"What's the worst that can happen?"* speech," said Steve.

"I vote for option four!" said Qwas.

"I wonder how Kapaloos taste best," I said. "Beer battered or charbroiled?'

"Ack!" said Qwas.

"Tastes like chicken," said Larry. Everyone looked at him. "Well that's what I heard."

"So how long until we'll know?" asked Nicole.

"It should just be a few moments," said Varcus.

We stood silently waiting for Varcus' PED to beep, an invisible clock slowly tick tocking in our heads.

"Anyone want to play Yahtzee?" said Larry.

"No!" said everyone, including those creatures that had no idea what he was talking about.

"And get your hands off me," said Nicole.

"Which one?" said Larry.

"All of them," said Nicole.

We waited what seemed like an eternity before Varcus' PED finally went off and he answered it. "So what's the verdict?" he said into it.

"Uh-huh," said Varcus.

"I see," said Varcus. "Really?"

"Are you positive? Okay," said Varcus. "I'll inform everyone and we'll get started on it right away."

"Yes, you too. Say hi to Mafie and the kids for me. Goodbye," said Varcus, and he pushed the end button and put his PED away.

"Well?" I asked.

"Well what?" asked Varcus.

"What do you think well what? What did they decide?" said Steve.

"Oh that," said Varcus. "We're moving you all back to Earth, of course."

"You are?" said Nicole.

"There was really nothing else we could do, was there?" asked Varcus. "We aren't going to let the Kapaloo die, and we can't legally move you humans off of Gork without your permission."

"What about option four?" asked Qwas, somewhat disappointed.

"They told me to try that," said Varcus. "They were hoping it would scare you all into backing off. You didn't think we'd actually do it, did you?"

"The thought crossed my mind, yes," said Steve.

"I'm amazed they came to a decision so quickly," said Nicole. "It would have taken months or years in one of our courts."

"But your courts are what made them make up their minds so quickly. It was bad enough we didn't have any options, but no one wanted to tangle with all your lawyers," said Varcus.

"So what happens now?" I said.

"First we'll have to put the parts of Washington D.C. we've removed back," said Varcus. "We wouldn't want you to lose any of your government."

"That would be a shame," I said. "And then?"

"Then we'll start transporting you back to Earth. Probably tomorrow afternoon," said Varcus. "So if you'll excuse me, I suddenly have a lot of work to do."

"Cool. Great. Go do your thing then," I said. Qwas and Varcus headed towards Varcus' ship. "Hey, will we see you back on Earth?"

"No!" said Qwas.

"Not you, Chihuahua man," I said.

"I'll be there," said Varcus, and he disappeared behind a row of trees.

"I suppose this means you won't honor the petition now?" asked Larry.

"You suppose right," I said.

"Dang it. And I was up to fourteen signatures," said Larry, and he wandered off to ask Paula for the umpteenth time if she was ready to forgive him yet.

"Nice going, counselor," said Steve. "You pulled it off after all."

"Yes, I'm impressed," said Nicole.

"He never stood a chance," I said. "That'll teach him to mess with a planet full of attorneys. And I guess that'll be the end of lawyer jokes back on Earth."

"I wouldn't go that far," said Nicole.

"I'm going to go tell Cynthia the good news," said Steve. "At least I think it's good news. She's been decorating our porta-potty home all day; hopefully she'll still want to move. Oh, and we definitely need to throw a party when we get back to Earth and celebrate."

Steve walked away and I stood there, feeling very pleased with myself, then scowled and shouted after him.

"You should tell them first!" I said, pointing at the crowd from New Glenbrook that were still standing nearby glaring at me. A person in the back of the group suddenly held up a homemade sign that read *"Jake Sux"* and waved it around.

"Yeah, I suck now," I said loudly to them. "Just wait 'till you're all back on Earth. You'll be naming babies after me."

"So did I hear there's a party on the horizon?" said Nicole.

"That's the rumor," I said.

"Do you suppose there'll be dancing?" said Nicole.

"There might be," I said. "Why do you ask?"

"I was thinking I might need a partner," said Nicole.

"It looked to me like you already have one," I said.

"Who, Larry? Hm. I suppose the two extra arms might come in handy during a tango. But I had someone else in mind," said Nicole.

"Anyone I know?" I said.

"Just some Representative guy," said Nicole.

"Sounds like a real loser to me," I said.

"Actually he's turning out to be okay," she said. "Come on; let's go get packed," she added, taking me by the hand and guiding me towards the shelters. "So do you think Varcus is ever going to figure out Johnny and Robb's scam?"

"You mean, Johnny contacting Robb and telling him what we needed, and Robb relaying orders to the moving bots and ships and rerouting them from Earth to here?" I asked.

"Yes that," said Nicole.

"Naw. Although there might be some guy in New Glenbrook wondering what the hell happened to his barbecue grill when he gets back to Earth," I said. "Hopefully the one waving that sign at me."

"I think all the stuff came from DC, though," said Nicole. "Remember? All the volleyballs had the presidential seal."

"That's right," I said. "I just hope it doesn't mean I'm going to get audited every year from now on."

Chapter Twenty Eight

Robb threw yet another ringer at the Anderson farm horseshoe pit, and he and Johnny celebrated as Varcus looked on.

"There you are. What's up, big guy?" I asked, as I handed him a cup of rum punch.

"Nothing is up," said Varcus somberly.

"You're not still sore about us humans being back on Earth, are you?" I said. Varcus looked at me and I immediately felt a big twinge of guilt. "I know, we kind of blackmailed you, but aren't you the least bit happy for us?"

"Of course I am; you're very nice beings. But this was bigger than you," said Varcus. "You know it's not always just about you humans you know."

"Yeah, but we're here now. And it's a beautiful Earth night, Steve and Cynthia are throwing this great barn dance slash luau, there's a great band; what's there to worry about?" I said.

Varcus gave me that look again, and I stopped smiling, feeling a wave of guilt the size of a tsunami wash over me. "I know, there's still the whole environmental thing. Look, I'm gonna do everything I can to make sure we get things working right here on Earth."

Varcus continued to stare at me, and I considered squirming for the first time in my life. "I mean it," I said instead, meaning it. "I've got this whole celebrity Representative thing going for me now, and I'm going to use it to fight eco evil doers."

"That makes me feel better, Jake," said Varcus. "I believe you'll do just that."

"Good," I said, suddenly feeling relieved. "You know, you should teach me that look you do. I could go around the planet getting CEOs to lower their company's emissions in a heartbeat."

"What look?" asked Varcus.

"That look you were just giving me. That *'you've been very, very, naughty and you should feel very, very, guilty about it'* look," I said.

"Oh that look," said Varcus, taking a drink of his punch. "To learn it you'd need to break your Vandorian mother's three hundred year old Actadel marriage vase playing womball in the house, and then try to blame it on your goofur."

"Never mind, then; I don't own a goofur," I said. "Let's go inside where the party is instead." We did so, and Varcus excused himself to go get a plate of roast pig and sweet corn.

I spied Larry looking gloomy over in the corner and went over to him.

"Now what's wrong with you?" I said.

Larry pointed at Tommy and Paula out on the dance floor. "What does he have that I don't have? Besides less manliness and arms."

I watched the two dance for a moment. "I don't know, but I'm pretty sure they're just friends, no matter what Tommy might be hoping for."

"In spite of my obvious superiority to him she won't have anything to do with me," said Larry sulkily. "I think she still wants me to sign a metaphysical exclusive rights agreement with her, so perhaps I will just give up on trying to woo her again. It would put too great a strain on the relationship between me and my libido to say goodbye to all the other chicks out there."

"Your choice. She's a pretty nice catch though," I said.

"Yes she is. But I think I like the fishing part better," said Larry. He looked off into the distance, and looked unhappy again.

"Now what?" I said. "Boy, you aliens are a moody bunch tonight. Robb is the only one in a good mood, and that's just plain weird."

"I was thinking about my pizza parlor," said Larry. "And how it won't be a pizza parlor now and will only be a planet instead."

"Can't you just do it without us?" I said.

"No. It's against interstellar copyright laws to make a profit from an original idea of an alien species," said Larry. "Having you humans live and work there would have made it legal, but now I would have to give the billions upon billions of pizzas away, and that would make earning back my setup costs most difficult. But it's the pizza I will miss the most. Kneading the floury dough with my hands, pouring on the rich red sauce as I slowly rotate the pan, sprinkling on the majestic cheese, carefully placing the thinly sliced spicy pepperoni in an eye pleasing pattern..." said Larry, becoming all misty eyed.

"Would you like to be alone with your pie?" I said.

"I will miss it all so much!" said Larry, starting to tear up.

"Look; and I can't believe I'm about to say this," I said. "I have an uncle back in Chicago who runs a little pizzeria around the corner from my place downtown; they make a great Chicago style pie. He's been wanting to get out of the business for some time now and move to Tampa where it's warm, but he's been having trouble finding a buyer with this economy. If you're interested I could get you two together and-"

"Me?! Buy a pizza place on Earth? That thought had never entered my overly large brain," said Larry. "I guess my thought patterns tend towards the really big ideas and miss out sometimes on the little smaller ideas that are actually more aesthetically pleasing and-"

"Yeah, yeah, yeah," I interrupted. "Would you be interested or not?"

"Yes," whimpered Larry happily, eyes full of tears. "Thank you!" he said, and wrapped all four arms around me before I could stop him, giving me a long and not so manly hug. "I must go outside now and hide my wet optic marbles before my chromosome patterns come under questioning," he said, and rushed out the door of the barn.

"I see you and Larry are bonding," said Nicole, coming up behind me. "How was the hug?"

"Disturbingly beguiling," I said. "I can unfortunately see now why women like those quadruple limbs of his."

"Should I be jealous?" asked Nicole.

"Maybe. I get the feeling I'm going to be seeing a lot of him in the future," I said worriedly.

"Dudes! You gotta see this," said Johnny, walking up with Robb. "Go ahead and show 'em, Robodude."

Robb put the skateboard he was carrying down on the wooden barn floor and stepped gingerly onto it. He crouched slowly and carefully, then jumped and tried to do an Ollie, but got tangled up in the landing and crashed to the ground with a loud clatter. "Ouch," he said.

"He's supposed to do that, right?" I said.

"What do you mean?" said Johnny. "Do what?"

"Fall down and hurt himself. I see you skater types do that all the time," I said.

"Yeah, it's part of the fun," said Johnny.

Robb got up and brushed himself off. "It's part of the fun I have not embraced quite yet."

"You'll have lots of time, dude," said Johnny. "Did you hear? Varcus said Robb can stay on Earth with me!"

"Really? How does your mom feel about that?" asked Nicole.

"She was pretty sore until Robb vacuumed the house, did the dishes and the laundry, and took out the garbage," said Johnny. "Now I think she wants to adopt him."

"Your birth parent is very nice," said Robb. "You should appreciate her more."

"Oh, Yeah? If you thought Varcus was bossy just wait," said Johnny. "Come on, let's go back outside. Those two old timers wanted to play another round of shoes, double or nothing."

"Alright, but I feel guilty about taking their money," said Robb.

"Do you want your own board or not?" asked Johnny, heading towards the door. "Hurry before they change their minds."

Varcus strolled up with a plate of food and a barbecue sauce goatee. "Has anyone seen Steve or

Cynthia? I simply must have this delicious roast mammal recipe."

"I think they're in the house," said Nicole.

"What, again?" I said. "Are they trying to set some sort of record?"

"They're newlyweds now," said Nicole.

"But they've been living together in sin for almost a year," I said. "It can't be that different."

"Cynthia did say something about her biological clock getting jump started with all this Earth and life talk," said Nicole.

"Oh sure. Varcus just gets finished putting all us messy humans back on the planet, and the first thing they want to do is manufacture more of us," I said.

"Yes," said Nicole.

"Speaking of manufactured beings I hear you ditched Robb, Varcus," I said.

"Um, yes," said Varcus. It's borderline illegal for me to leave him here, but it's what he wanted."

"Well, it was borderline illegal for you to leave us here too," I said. "Hey, does this make us all illegal aliens now?"

"I suppose it does," said Varcus.

"Cool," I said.

Larry came back inside and stood next to me, striking his manliest pose.

"All better now?" I asked.

"Yes, thank you," said Larry.

"Would you like to dance?" asked Nicole.

"Sure!" said Larry happily.

"Not you, Larry!" said Nicole, exasperated with him by now. "I meant Jake."

"How about a rain check?" I said. "I've been meaning to ask Larry here something."

"Alright. Varcus?" said Nicole.

"It would be my pleasure," said Varcus, and he presented an arm for Nicole to take. She did so, and they disappeared onto the crowded dance floor, except for Varcus' head and shoulders, of course.

"What did you want to ask me, best buddy?" asked Larry.

"Best buddy?" I said.

"Yes," said Larry. "I was thinking since I am going to be working in the neighborhood where you live we can be BFFLs and do all sorts of manly things together, like go to football games, drink beer, pick up chicks, go to the bingo hall..."

"We'll see about that. Anyway, I've been wondering," I said. "And since we're suddenly best friends maybe you can level with me. Your planet, Aurora. Was it really as nice as it looked?"

"Yes. Definitely," said Larry.

"Really?" I said skeptically.

"Really," said Larry. "That one island, anyway."

"That's what I thought," I said.

"On the one side," said Larry.

"Uh-huh," I said.

"Especially after I changed the color of the sky in the 6D video," said Larry. "And of the water. And added that second sun. And tweaked the temperature about thirty degrees."

"Yep," I said.

"And turned all the plague carrying mega-skeeters buzzing around into pretty birds," said Larry.

"Ever thought about going into real estate?" I asked.

"Naw," said Larry. "Not enough oregano."

Chapter Twenty Nine

Nicole, Cynthia, and I, stood in the driveway next to Steve's fully decorated *"Just Married"* pick-up truck, a *"Wisconsin Dells or bust!"* sign in the back window. Cynthia gave Nicole a hug, then walked over to me and gave me a big long squeeze. "Thanks, Jake; for everything," she said.

"No problem, girlfriend," I said, and Cynthia went around and got in the truck.

Steve reached out the window and we shook hands. "See ya, buddy. Nicole's got the key; just lock up and put it in the milk can when you're ready to leave. You guys can stay as long as you want."

"Thanks. I can use a vacation after all that," I said. "You guys have a good time. But keep him out of the sun, Cynthia. He burns in like two and a half minutes."

Cynthia smiled and Steve waved and put the truck into gear, and they drove away down the road.

"Better go say bye to the big guy," I said. "You want to come?"

"Varcus and I already said our goodbyes," said Nicole. "Besides, you two should be alone anyway in case you want to get all mushy."

I walked across the yard and up to the top of the ramp of the ship, where Varcus was standing waving to Steve and Cynthia.

"Great party last night, Jake," said Varcus. "Was Cynthia upset about her cows?"

"A little, but lucky for you she was too excited about the honeymoon to do anything about it," I said.

"I'm sorry anyway. I guess I got carried away," said Varcus.

"Is their milk going to be colored too?" I asked. "You know, green from the green cows, pink from the pink cows, etc."

"I'm afraid so," said Varcus. "But it won't affect the taste. And it should wear off in a few days. Or maybe weeks; hopefully not months."

"Hey, don't sweat it. That's what cows are for; milking, eating and abusing," I said.

"Evidently," said Varcus. "I see Larry is gone. Did he go home?"

"Yeah, he went to get his things, especially his lucky oven mitt," I said.

"Good old Larry," said Varcus. "Having him in your neighborhood should prove most interesting."

"That's one way to put it," I said.

We fell silent for a moment, and looked at one another. "We've come far, you and me," said Varcus.

"Yes we have," I said. "Hey wait a minute, where have I heard that before?"

Varcus sighed. "Okay, it's from *Dances with Wolves*," he admitted. "You know, at the end? Where Kicking Bird is talking to Dances with Wolves."

"Right; that's it. Great movie," I said.

"Great screenplay. Michael Blake. I just always wanted to say it," said Varcus. "But this is it I guess. It's been-"

"Educational," I finished.

"I hope so. Take care," said Varcus. He put out a giant hand towards me and I gladly took it and shook it, then he suddenly grabbed me and gave me the manliest hug of my life.

"You take care too, Varcus," I said once I was finally set free. "If you're ever in the neighborhood, give me a call; we'll catch a Cubs game. You, me, and Larry."

"I'll do that. Goodbye, Jake," said Varcus, and he stepped inside his ship, and I walked down the ramp, then stopped at the bottom and turned.

"Hey, are you gonna do that time travel thing again?" I shouted. "Jump ahead ten, twenty years, and see what happens to us?"

Varcus stuck his head back outside the door. "No, I think I'll stick around the area for a while this time. I want to see what your people can do."

"Me too," I said. I walked over to Nicole, and we stood watching and waving as Varcus' ship glided silently up into the blue sky and disappeared.

Nicole looked around at the farm, which suddenly looked surprisingly ordinary, except for the herd of rainbow colored bovines. "Alone at last."

"Yep. Not an alien in sight," I said.

"No, there isn't. So what now?" asked Nicole.

"What now?" I said. "Now I think I'm going to take a look at environmental law. And you've got a few photos to show to someone."

"That sounds great," said Nicole. "But that's not what I meant."

"Well, what did you mean?" I said.

"I meant right now, now. What should we do now?" said Nicole.

I thought about it for a moment. "I don't know about you, but I could really go for some pizza."

"I am famished," said Nicole. "Do you want to drive?"

I put my arm around Nicole's waist and looked at the beautiful Earth day. "Naw," I said. "Let's walk."

And we did.

Made in the USA
Lexington, KY
30 April 2013